TEXAS

United States History

EARLY COLONIAL PERIOD

THROUGH RECONSTRUCTION

Guided Reading
Workbook

Houghton Mifflin Harcourt

ISBN 978-0-544-32990-4

4 5 6 7 8 9 10 0982   23 22 21 20 19 18 17 16 15

4500536225 A B C D E F G

Contents

The Nation Breaks Apart

How to Use this Book

The *Guided Reading Workbook* was developed to help you get the most from your reading. Using this book will help you master United States history content while developing your reading and vocabulary skills. Reviewing the next few pages before getting started will make you aware of the many useful features in this book.

Section summary pages allow you to interact with the content and key terms and places from each section of a chapter. The summaries explain each section of your textbook in a way that is easy to understand.

Section numbers make it easy to find your place in the workbook.

The main idea statements help focus your attention as you read the summaries.

Definitions for the key terms and people from your textbook are given.

Headings under each section summary match those of your textbook, which can help you find the material you need.

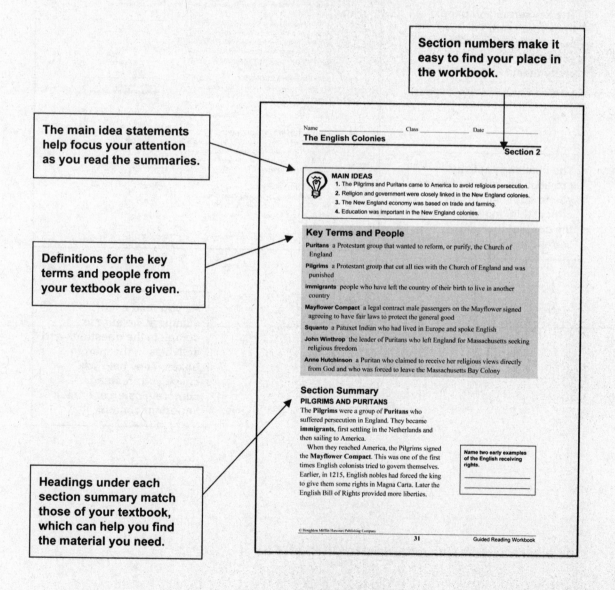

Name _____ Class _____ Date _____

The English Colonies

Section 2

MAIN IDEAS
1. The Pilgrims and Puritans came to America to avoid religious persecution.
2. Religion and government were closely linked in the New England colonies.
3. The New England economy was based on trade and farming.
4. Education was important in the New England colonies.

Key Terms and People

Puritans a Protestant group that wanted to reform, or purify, the Church of England

Pilgrims a Protestant group that cut all ties with the Church of England and was punished

immigrants people who have left the country of their birth to live in another country

Mayflower Compact a legal contract male passengers on the Mayflower signed agreeing to have fair laws to protect the general good

Squanto a Patuxet Indian who had lived in Europe and spoke English

John Winthrop the leader of Puritans who left England for Massachusetts seeking religious freedom

Anne Hutchinson a Puritan who claimed to receive her religious views directly from God and who was forced to leave the Massachusetts Bay Colony

Section Summary

PILGRIMS AND PURITANS

The **Pilgrims** were a group of **Puritans** who suffered persecution in England. They became **immigrants**, first settling in the Netherlands and then sailing to America.

When they reached America, the Pilgrims signed the **Mayflower Compact**. This was one of the first times English colonists tried to govern themselves. Earlier, in 1215, English nobles had forced the king to give them some rights in Magna Carta. Later the English Bill of Rights provided more liberties.

Name two early examples of the English receiving rights.

_____

_____

© Houghton Mifflin Harcourt Publishing Company

31

Guided Reading Workbook

The key terms and people from your textbook have been boldfaced, allowing you to quickly find and study them.

The challenge activity provides an opportunity for you to apply important critical thinking skills using the content that you learned in the section.

Name _____ Class _____ Date _____
Section 2, *continued*

The Pilgrims learned to fertilize their soil from **Squanto**. They invited him and 90 Wampanoag guests to a feast now known as Thanksgiving.

Religion and education played important parts in the Pilgrims' lives, which centered on families. Everyone worked hard. Women had rights that they did not have in England.

Puritans and merchants founded the Massachusetts Bay colony. Tens of thousands of English men, women and children would immigrate to it. **John Winthrop** led one group. Puritans believe they had a sacred agreement with God to build a Christian colony.

> What was the Puritans' sacred agreement with God?
> _____
> _____

RELIGION AND GOVERNMENT IN NEW ENGLAND

Politics and religion were closely linked in Puritan New England. Some self-government existed. However, only the chosen male church members could vote.

Some Puritans had different religious views than others. Minister Roger Williams supported the separation of the church from politics. He founded Providence. **Anne Hutchinson** was forced to leave the colony because of her religious ideas.

> Underline the sentence that means women could not vote in Puritan New England.

NEW ENGLAND ECONOMY

The New England colonies had a hard climate and rocky soil. The kind of farming done in Virginia was impossible there. Instead, they traded goods, fished, built ships, and became skilled craftspeople.

> Compare sources of income in Virginia and New England.
> _____
> _____

EDUCATION IN THE COLONIES

New England parents wanted their children to read the Bible. They made laws requiring the education of children. The colonists also founded Harvard College to teach ministers.

CHALLENGE ACTIVITY

Critical Thinking: Developing Questions
Develop three questions about the Pilgrims' contributions and research to answer them.

32   Guided Reading Workbook

As you read each summary, be sure to complete the questions and activities in the margin boxes. They help you check your reading comprehension and track important content.

The third page of each section allows you to demonstrate your understanding of the key terms and people introduced in the section.

Some pages have a word bank. You can use it to help find answers or complete writing activities.

Various activities help you check your knowledge of key terms and people.

Writing activities require you to include key terms and people in what you write. Remember to check to make sure that you are using the terms and names correctly.

Name _____ Class _____ Date _____
Section 2, *continued*

Anne Hutchinson	John Winthrop	Pilgrims
immigrants	Mayflower Compact	Puritans
Squanto		

DIRECTIONS Answer each question by writing a sentence that contains at least one word from the word bank.

1. Who was put on trial for his or her religious ideas and eventually forced out of the colony?

_____

_____

2. Who are people that leave their country of birth to live in another country?

_____

_____

3. Who showed the Pilgrims how to fertilize the soil on their farms and helped them establish relations with the chief of the local Wampanoag Indians?

_____

_____

4. Who led a group of Puritan colonists who left England for Massachusetts in search of religious freedom?

_____

_____

5. What Protestant group wanted to reform, or purify, the Church of England?

_____

_____

DIRECTIONS Choose at least five of the vocabulary words from the word bank. On a separate sheet of paper, use these words to write a letter that relates to the section.

© Houghton Mifflin Harcourt Publishing Company

33   Guided Reading Workbook

The World before the Opening of the Atlantic

MAIN IDEAS

1. Climate changes allowed Paleo-Indians to begin the first migration to the Americas.
2. Early societies existed in Mesoamerica and South America.

Key Terms and People

Bering Land Bridge a strip of land between Asia and present-day Alaska that was exposed by the lower sea levels of the Ice Age

Paleo-Indians people believed to have crossed the Bering Land Bridge

migration movement of people or animals from one region to another

hunter-gatherers people who obtain food by hunting animals and gathering plants

environments climates and landscapes that surround living things

culture a group's set of common values and traditions

Academic Vocabulary

develop the process of growing or improving

Section Summary

FIRST MIGRATION TO THE AMERICAS

Many scientists believe that the first people arrived in North America during the last Ice Age. At that time the **environment** changed, and large amounts of water froze, forming glaciers. Water levels in the oceans dropped to more than 300 feet lower than they are today. A strip of land called the **Bering Land Bridge** was exposed between Asia and Alaska.

No one knows exactly when or how people crossed into North America, but there is evidence that people called **Paleo-Indians** crossed the bridge to Alaska between 38,000 and 10,000 BC. The **migration** took place over a long time. The descendents of the migrants went as far as the southern tip of South America. These people were **hunter-gatherers,** people who hunted animals and gathered wild plants for food. The environments they settled in created Native American societies.

> How did the formation of glaciers during the Ice Age allow for migration to North America?
>
> _____
> _____
> _____

> Do scientists know exactly when the Paleo-Indians crossed into North America?
>
> _____
> _____
> _____

EARLY MESOAMERICAN AND SOUTH AMERICAN SOCIETIES

Some of the earliest American **cultures** arose in Mesoamerica, a region that includes the southern part of what is now Mexico and northern Central America. The Olmec **developed** the earliest known civilization in Mesoamerica around 1200 BC. The Olmec are known for their stone buildings and sculptures. By 400 BC, when their civilization ended, trade had spread Olmec **culture.**

The Maya civilization followed the Olmec. The Maya built large stone temples, pyramids, and canals that controlled the flow of water through their cities. The Maya civilization began to collapse in the 900s, but historians are still not sure why.

The Aztec were fierce warriors who migrated to south and central Mexico in the mid-1100s. They conquered many towns, built a large empire, and controlled a huge trading network. The Aztec capital, Tenochtitlán (tay-nawch-teet-LAHN), founded in 1325 AD, became the greatest city in the Americas and one of the world's largest cities. The Aztec became rich on trade and tributes paid by conquered people.

The Inca began as a small tribe in the Andes Mountains. In the mid-1400s, the Inca began expanding their empire until it included much of the western coast of South America and had more than 12 million people. The Inca people had a strong central government and a network of roads and bridges that connected all parts of the territory.

Underline the sentence that tells when the first civilization developed in Mesoamerica.

What evidence do we have that cultures existed in Mesoamerica before the Aztecs? _____ _____ _____

What was the greatest city in the Americas during the height of the Aztec culture? _____ _____

CHALLENGE ACTIVITY

Critical Thinking: Evaluate Imagine that you lived in Mesoamerica or South America before the arrival of Europeans. Write a short paragraph describing which of the four civilizations discussed above you would have preferred to live in. Be sure to support your answer.

| migration | culture | environment |
| Bering Land Bridge | hunter-gatherers | Paleo-Indians |

DIRECTIONS On the line provided before each statement, write **T** if a statement is true or **F** if a statement is false. If the statement is false, find a word or phrase in the word bank that makes the statement true. Write a new sentence on the line provided.

_____ 1. <u>Culture</u> is the movement of people or animals from one region to another.

_____

_____ 2. <u>Migration</u> is the climate and landscapes that surround living things.

_____

_____ 3. <u>Paleo-Indians</u> crossed the Bering Land Bridge into Alaska between 38,000 and 10,000 BC.

_____

_____ 4. A group's set of common values and traditions is called a <u>Bering Land Bridge</u>.

_____

_____ 5. Paleo-Indians were <u>hunter-gatherers</u> who lived by hunting animals and gathering wild plants.

_____

_____ 6. The <u>culture</u> was a strip of solid land believed to have once connected Siberia and present-day Alaska.

_____

Guided Reading Workbook

The World before the Opening of the Atlantic

Section 2

MAIN IDEAS
1. Several early societies developed in North America long before Europeans explored the continent.
2. Geographic areas influenced Native American cultures.
3. Native American cultures shared beliefs about religion and land ownership.

Key Terms and People

pueblos aboveground houses made of a heavy clay called adobe

kivas underground ceremonial chambers at the center of each Anasazi community

totems ancestor or animal spirits of the Native Americans of the Pacific Northwest

teepees cone-shaped shelters made of animal hides by the nomadic plains people

matrilineal a society that traces ancestry through mothers

Iroquois League an alliance of Native Americans in northeastern North America

Section Summary

EARLY SOCIETIES

The earliest people in North America were hunter-gatherers. By 1500 BC people in the southwestern part of North America had farm cultures and grew maize. The Anasazi used irrigation to increase food production in the dry climate. They lived in pit houses dug into the ground and later began to build **pueblos.** The Anasazi often built complex houses on cliff walls to defend against attacks. They also built **kivas,** sacred areas at the center of the community.

The Anasazi began abandoning their villages after living in them for hundreds of years. Drought, disease, or raids by other tribes may have caused this move.

After 1000 BC several farming societies developed in the eastern part of North America. They built large burial mounds to honor their dead. More than 10,000 mounds have been found in the Ohio River valley alone. The largest city of the mound builders had about 30,000 people.

> **How would building on cliff walls provide protection for the Anasazi?**
> _____
> _____
> _____

> **Why would drought be one of the possible reasons that the Anasazi moved from their homes?**
> _____
> _____
> _____

Guided Reading Workbook

NATIVE AMERICAN CULTURE AREAS

The culture of Native American people varied depending on geography. In the far north, in present-day Alaska and Canada, Native Americans survived primarily by hunting and fishing, living in small groups. Farther south, along the Pacific Northwest, larger groups thrived on the abundant wildlife. They carved tall poles with **totems**—symbols of animal or ancestor spirits—which had religious and cultural meaning.

Farther south along the Pacific and the Sierra Nevada Mountains, people fished, hunted, gathered plants, and lived in small groups of families. In the drier areas of the southwest, Pueblo groups had to develop agriculture to adapt to the climate. They lived in towns of up to 1000 people. Others, such as the Apache and Navajo, formed nomadic groups that survived by hunting, foraging, or raiding other villages.

Most of the Native Americans of the Great Plains were nomadic hunters. They survived on the abundant wildlife of the grasslands, living in **teepees** made of animal hides. Some Plains groups were farmers, including the Pawnee, who had a **matri-lineal** society. In the east, many Native Americans had small villages and lived by farming, hunting, and fishing. The **Iroquois League** was an alliance of many groups that defended one another.

SHARED BELIEFS

Although they had many different cultures, Native Americans shared certain beliefs. Their religions were linked to nature, and they believed that the land was for the use of everyone.

CHALLENGE ACTIVITY

Critical Thinking: Comparing Pick two Native American groups from two different culture areas. Make a chart comparing these two societies.

> What was the significance of the characters carved on totem poles?
>
> _____
>
> _____
>
> _____

> Describe the food and shelter of the Native Americans of the Great Plains.
>
> _____
>
> _____
>
> _____

Guided Reading Workbook

DIRECTIONS Write two adjectives or descriptive phrases that describe the term.

1. Iroquois League _____

2. kivas _____

3. matrilineal _____

4. pueblos _____

5. teepees _____

6. totems _____

DIRECTIONS Read each sentence and fill in the blank with the word in the word pair that best completes the sentence.

7. _____ are cone shaped shelters. (kivas/teepees)

8. Pawnee society was _____, which means that people traced their ancestry through their mothers, not their fathers. (matrilineal/totems)

9. After about AD 750 the Anasazi built _____, or aboveground houses made of heavy clay called adobe. (pueblos/kivas)

10. Native Americans in the Pacific Northwest carved images of ancestor or animal spirits called _____ on tall, wooden polls. (totems/teepees)

The World before the Opening of the Atlantic

MAIN IDEAS
1. West Africa developed three great kingdoms that grew wealthy through their control of trade.
2. Slaves became a valuable trade item in West Africa.

Key Terms and People

Berbers North African people who established trade routes through West Africa

Mansa Musa a Muslim king who ruled the Mali Empire at the height of its power and who spread Islamic influence through a large part of West Africa

hajj in Islam, a pilgrimage to the holy city of Mecca

mosques Islamic places of worship

Askia the Great the Muslim ruler who led Songhai to the height of its power

Section Summary

WEST AFRICA'S GREAT KINGDOMS

West African trade routes were originally controlled by the **Berbers,** a people of North Africa. Later, three great kingdoms developed in West Africa by winning control of these trade routes.

The first, Ghana, formed when farmers banded together to protect themselves from herders. They built armies whose superior iron weapons let them take control of the trade in salt and gold. Ghana raised money by forcing traders who passed through its lands to pay taxes. The trade routes brought Ghana in contact with different cultures and beliefs. In the 1060s a Muslim group attacked Ghana, forcing its leaders to convert to Islam. Although Ghana was weakened and eventually fell, the influence of Islam remained strong.

Like Ghana, Mali was located along the upper Niger River. The fertile soil and the control of trade on the river allowed Mali to become rich and powerful. Its most famous ruler was a Muslim king, **Mansa Musa.** Under his leadership Mali grew in wealth and power. Traders came to Timbuktu, an

> What was the main source of the wealth and power of all the West African empires?
>
> _____
> _____
> _____

> What river flowed through both Ghana and Mali?
>
> _____
> _____

important city, to trade for salt, gold, metals, shells, and other goods.

Because he was a devout Muslim, Mansa Musa left Mali on a **hajj,** or a pilgrimage to Mecca. His influence helped bring Islam to a large part of West Africa. In the 1300s Mansa Musa conquered a kingdom called Songhai, whose people also lived along the Niger River. As the Mali empire weakened in the 1400s, Songhai regained independence.

One of the greatest Songhai rulers was Muhammad Ture. He chose a military title, *askia,* and became known as **Askia the Great.** Like Mansa Musa, Askia was a devout Muslim who supported education and learning. His cities had great **mosques,** schools, and libraries. He built a professional army and organized Songhai with governors who were loyal to him. Songhai declined soon after Askia the Great lost power.

> What did Mansa Musa and Askia the Great have in common?
>
> _____
> _____
> _____

WEST AFRICAN SLAVE TRADE

Slavery had existed in Africa and in many parts of the world for centuries. Starting in the 600s Arabs and then Europeans became slave traders. Criminals and people captured during battle could be sold into slavery as well as relatives of people who owed money.

> Underline the sentence that explains how it was determined who would become a slave in West Africa.

The market for West African slaves increased as Muslim traders took black Africans to sell in North Africa. West Africa was also the home of many slaves taken to the Americas. The slave trade became a key part of the West African economy, contributing to the power of the great empires.

CHALLENGE ACTIVITY

Critical Thinking: Elaborate Imagine that you live in one of the kingdoms discussed in this section. Write a brief description of what an average day might be like.

Askia the Great	hajj	mosques
Berbers	Mansa Musa	

DIRECTIONS On the line provided before each statement, write **T** if a
statement is true or **F** if a statement is false. If the statement is false,
find a word or phrase in the word bank that makes the statement true.
Write the new sentence on the line provided.

_____ 1. For hundreds of years, West Africans did not profit much from the
Saharan trade because the routes were run by <u>mosques</u>.

_____

_____

_____ 2. Mali reached the height of its wealth, power, and fame under <u>Askia the
Great</u>.

_____

_____

_____ 3. With religion being very important to Mansa Musa, he left Mali in 1324
on a <u>hajj</u>.

_____

_____

_____ 4. Mansa Musa began building <u>mosques</u>, which were used for Muslim
prayer.

_____

_____

_____ •5. <u>Askia the Great</u> supported education and learning and created an effective
government.

_____

_____

The World before the Opening of the Atlantic

MAIN IDEAS

1. The Greeks and Romans established new forms of government.
2. During the Middle Ages, society eventually changed from a feudal system to the development of a middle class of artisans and merchants.
3. The Renaissance created a rebirth of arts and learning.

Key Terms and People

Socrates Greek teacher who wanted people to question their own beliefs

Plato Greek philosopher who wrote *Republic*, about an ideal society

Aristotle Greek philosopher who thought people should live based on reason

reason clear or ordered thinking

democracy a form of government in which people rule themselves

knights feudal warriors who fought on horseback

Black Death a disease that spread across Europe, killing 25 million people

Michelangelo Italian Renaissance artist known for paintings and sculpture

Leonardo da Vinci Italian artist, inventor, engineer, and mapmaker of the Renaissance

Johannes Gutenberg German inventor of the moveable type printing press

joint-stock companies businesses in which a group of people invest together

Academic Vocabulary

classical referring to the cultures of ancient Greece and Rome

Section Summary

GREEK AND ROMAN GOVERNMENT

Ancient Greeks valued human reason and believed in the power of the human mind to think, explain, and understand life. Three of the greatest Greek thinkers were **Socrates, Plato,** and **Aristotle,** who were all philosophers and teachers. Aristotle taught that people should live lives based on **reason,** or clear and ordered thinking.

One of the most lasting contributions of the Greeks is their political system. Established during the **Classical** Period, **democracy** is the system in

> Who were three of the greatest Greek thinkers?
>
> _____
> _____
> _____

> Underline the sentence that describes the Greek contribution of a political system.

which people rule themselves. Rome later formed a type of democracy called a republic, in which people elect representatives to rule them. These political ideas still influence world governments, including that of the United States.

MIDDLE AGES

After the fall of the Roman empire, Europe was divided into many small kingdoms. A system called feudalism was established in which nobles gave **knights** land in exchange for protection.

In the 1000s important changes began to occur in Europe. The Crusades brought trade with places outside Europe, introducing new products and ideas. Trade also brought a disease known as the **Black Death** that killed much of the population of Europe and caused a shortage of workers. These changes resulted in the development of a middle-class made up of artisans and merchants. Cities became important as commercial centers for trade.

> How did the Black Death cause changes in commerce?
>
> _____
>
> _____
>
> _____

RENAISSANCE

The key feature of the Renaissance was a love of art and education. The search for knowledge spread to all fields. During the Renaissance the focus shifted from religion to people. Two of the great Renaissance artists, **Michelangelo** and **Leonardo da Vinci,** are famous for their paintings, sculpture, and architecture, which reflected the value of the human being. The printing press developed by **Johannes Gutenberg** helped spread new ideas in science, math, and literature.

> Underline the key feature of the Renaissance.

Increased trade caused a commercial revolution. Italian cities became important trading centers. As commerce grew, so did the need for banks. Merchants created **joint-stock companies** in which groups of people invested together.

> What helped spread new ideas during the Renaissance?
>
> _____
>
> _____
>
> _____

CHALLENGE ACTIVITY

Critical Thinking: Evaluate Make a chart showing some of democracy's advantages.

DIRECTIONS Look at each set of four vocabulary terms following each number. On the line provided, write the letter of the term that does not relate to the other terms.

_____ 1. a. Socrates
   b. Aristotle
   c. knights
   d. Plato

_____ 2. a. The Black Death
   b. Leonardo da Vinci
   c. joint-stock companies
   d. Johannes Gutenberg

DIRECTIONS Read each sentence and fill in the blank with the word in the word pair that best completes the sentence.

3. _____ wrote a work called *Republic*. (Aristotle/Plato)

4. The form of government in which people rule themselves is called

_____. (reason/democracy)

5. Aristotle taught _____, or clear and ordered thinking, as a

basis on which people should live their lives. (classical/reason)

6. Europe's economy declined dramatically after the _____

killed an estimated 25 million people. (knights/Black Death)

7. After _____ invented the printing press, thousands of people

began reading the same books. (Johannes Gutenberg/Socrates)

New Empires in the Americas

Section 1

 MAIN IDEAS

1. Vikings were skilled sailors, and they were the first Europeans to reach North America.
2. Prince Henry the Navigator established a school for sailors and provided financial support that enabled the Portuguese to start exploring the oceans.
3. Portuguese sailors sailed around Africa and found a sea route to Asia.

Key Terms and People

Leif Eriksson Viking who landed in present-day Canada in AD1000

Henry the Navigator Portuguese prince who established a school of navigation and paid for expeditions

astrolabe a device used to determine location based on the position of the stars

caravels Portuguese ships that used triangular sails to sail against the wind

Academic Vocabulary

effect the result of an action or decision

Section Summary

VIKING SAILORS REACH NORTH AMERICA

The Vikings were the first Europeans to make contact with North America. They were skilled sailors who developed a new style of ship that was more stable on rough seas.

In the year 1000, **Leif Eriksson,** the son of Erik the Red, set off for Greenland. Strong winds blew his ship off course, and he landed on the North American coast. The Vikings settled in a coastal area that Eriksson called Vinland, but they left after a few years. Europeans did not return to the continent for centuries.

> Who were the first Europeans to settle in North America?
> _____
> _____

PRINCE HENRY THE NAVIGATOR

In the early 1400s Portugal became a leader in world exploration. Although he never set out on a voyage himself, Prince **Henry the Navigator** helped Portugal's explorers succeed. He built an

> What European country led world exploration in the early 1400s?
> _____
> _____

observatory and a school of navigation to teach better methods of sailing. Europeans had several reasons to explore the world. They wanted spices from Asia, and they wanted to learn more about Asia and its culture. They also wanted to convert Asians to the Christian faith.

European sailors were able to travel in open seas without landmarks to guide them because of new technology. The **astrolabe** was used to chart a ship's location based on the position of the stars. The **caravel** was a new kind of ship that was smaller, lighter, and easier to steer. Caravels used triangular sails that allowed ships to sail against the wind and rudders that improved steering.

Why did Europeans want to explore the world?
_____
_____

A SEA ROUTE TO ASIA

In the 1400s Portuguese sailors traveled south along the coast of Africa, setting up trading posts along the way. In 1497 a Portuguese expedition led by Vasco da Gama sailed around the southern tip of Africa and reached India. These successful voyages had a number of **effects**, both positive and negative. Portugal's wealth and power increased. However, these travels eventually led to the spread of the slave trade. Other European nations soon began looking for their own sea routes to Asia.

What was the first sea route from Europe to Asia?
_____
_____

CHALLENGE ACTIVITY

Critical Thinking: Making Inferences The Portuguese had laws that included severe penalties for letting sailors from other countries see the maps the Portuguese created from their expeditions. Write a paragraph explaining why they wanted to keep these maps secret.

DIRECTIONS Look at each set of terms below. On the line provided, write the letter of the term that does not relate to the others.

_____ 1. a. Portuguese
     b. smaller, lighter, and easier to steer ships
     c. Vikings
     d. caravels

_____ 2. a. astrolabe
     b. new type of ship
     c. ship's location
     d. charted the position of the stars

_____ 3. a. Leif Eriksson
     b. caravel
     c. Henry the Navigator
     d. exploration

_____ 4. a. Portugal
     b. Prince Henry the Navigator
     c. observatory
     d. Viking

_____ 5. a. magnetic compass
     b. Leif Eriksson
     c. Vikings
     d. Erik the Red

_____ 6. a. longships
     b. Vikings
     c. caravels
     d. galleons

New Empires in the Americas

 MAIN IDEAS
1. Christopher Columbus sailed across the Atlantic Ocean and reached a continent that was previously unknown to him.
2. After Columbus's voyages, other explorers sailed to the Americas.

Key Terms and People

Christopher Columbus a sailor from Genoa, Italy

Line of Demarcation an imaginary boundary in the Atlantic dividing Spanish and Portuguese territories

Treaty of Tordesillas agreement between Spain and Portugal moving the Line of Demarcation

Ferdinand Magellan Portuguese navigator whose expedition circumnavigated the globe

circumnavigate to go all the way around the globe

Columbian Exchange the transfer of plants and animals between the Americas and Asia, Africa, and Europe

Section Summary
COLUMBUS SAILS ACROSS THE ATLANTIC

Christopher Columbus, a sailor from Genoa, Italy, believed that he could reach Asia by sailing west across the Atlantic Ocean. He asked King Ferdinand and Queen Isabella of Spain to pay for an expedition. In return, he promised great riches, new territory, and Catholic converts.

Sailing with three ships, Columbus reached an island in the Bahamas in 1492. Columbus thought he had found a new route to Asia. In reality he had reached another continent that was unknown to him. Columbus made three more journeys to the Americas during his lifetime. When he died in 1506 he still believed that he had reached Asia.

The voyages of Columbus changed the way Europeans saw the world and also created conflict between European nations. In 1493 the pope issued

> Why did the Spanish and other Europeans want to find a route to Asia?
> _____
> _____
> _____

> Underline the sentence that explains where Columbus thought he had landed.

a decree that created the **Line of Demarcation.**
This imaginary boundary divided the Atlantic
Ocean between Spain and Portugal. The Portuguese
king believed the arrangement favored Spain, so the
leaders of the two nations signed the **Treaty of
Tordesillas.** This treaty moved the Line of
Demarcation 800 miles further west and prevented a
war between the two countries.

> **What was the purpose of the Treaty of Tordesillas?**
> _____
> _____
> _____

OTHER EXPLORERS SAIL TO THE AMERICAS

After Columbus other explorers sailed across the
Atlantic Ocean. In 1501 Amerigo Vespucci became
convinced that he had not reached Asia but had
discovered a "new world." A German mapmaker
labeled the continents across the ocean as *America*
in his honor.

Vasco Núñez de Balboa, a Spanish explorer,
crossed the jungles of Central America to see the
Pacific Ocean in 1513. In 1519 Portuguese
navigator **Ferdinand Magellan** sailed around the
southern tip of South America and into the Pacific.
Although Magellan was killed in the Philippine
Islands, one ship from his expedition was the first to
circumnavigate, or go all the way around, the
globe.

> **Why do people say that Ferdinand Magellan circumnavigated the globe even though he died on the way?**
> _____
> _____
> _____

European explorers and settlers took plants and
animals with them to America and brought back
American plants and animals. This transfer was
called the **Columbian Exchange** because it started
with the explorations of Columbus. Over time a
trading pattern developed, involving the exchange
of raw materials, manufactured products, and slaves
among Europe, Africa, and the Americas.

CHALLENGE ACTIVITY

Critical Thinking: Elaborating Imagine you are a
sailor on one of Columbus's ships. Write a short
poem about the first sighting of land in the present-
day Bahamas.

Christopher Columbus	circumnavigate	Columbian Exchange
diseases	Ferdinand Magellan	King Ferdinand
Line of Demarcation	Queen Isabella I	Taino
Treaty of Tordesillas	Atlantic Ocean	Pacific Ocean

DIRECTIONS Choose five of the terms or people from the word bank.
Use the words to write an email message to your friend explaining what
you learned in the section.

_____

_____

_____

_____

_____

_____

_____

_____

_____

_____

_____

_____

_____

_____

_____

_____

New Empires in the Americas

Section 3

> **MAIN IDEAS**
> 1. Spanish conquistadors conquered the Aztec and Inca empires.
> 2. Spanish explorers traveled through the borderlands of New Spain, claiming more land.
> 3. Spanish settlers treated Native Americans harshly, forcing them to work on plantations and in mines.

Key Terms and People

conquistadors Spanish soldiers who led military expeditions in the Americas

Hernán Cortés conquistador who conquered the Aztec empire

Moctezuma II ruler of the Aztec empire

Francisco Pizarro a conquistador who captured the Inca capital and killed the Inca leaders

encomienda system a system that gave settlers the right to tax Native Americans or to make them work

plantations large farms that grew just one kind of crop and made huge profits for their owners

Bartolomé de Las Casas a priest who encouraged better treatment of Native Americans

Section Summary
SPANISH CONQUISTADORS

The Spanish sent **conquistadors** to the Americas on military expeditions. Conquistador **Hernán Cortés** went to present-day Mexico in 1519. He had heard of land to the west ruled by **Moctezuma II,** the king of the Aztec empire. The Spaniards believed the Aztec lands were a rich source of gold and silver. They also wanted to convert the Aztec to Christianity.

Although they were greatly outnumbered, the conquistadors had superior weapons and formed alliances with enemies of the Aztec. Cortés took control of the Aztec capital and killed Moctezuma. Smallpox and other European diseases sped up the fall of the Aztec empire.

> **Why might Cortés have wanted to conquer the Aztec?**
> _____
> _____
> _____

> **What advantage did the Spanish have over the Aztec?**
> _____
> _____

While seeking gold **Francisco Pizarro** led his troops to capture the great Inca capital at Cuzco. Within a few years Pizarro had conquered the entire Inca empire. The Spanish then began to create a vast empire which they called New Spain. They established settlements to serve as trading posts, missions to convert local Native Americans to Catholicism, and military bases.

> **Why did Pizarro first enter the Inca empire?**
>
> _____
>
> _____

EXPLORING THE BORDERLANDS OF NEW SPAIN

Spain's empire in America extended well beyond the lands taken from the Aztec and Inca. Regions claimed by the Spanish explorers included the island of Puerto Rico, the coast of present-day Florida, and the coastal regions of the Gulf of Mexico. The Spanish also explored what is now the southwestern United States, looking for cities of gold that were rumored to exist there. They traveled through unclaimed areas of Texas, Oklahoma, and as far north as Kansas.

SPANISH TREATMENT OF NATIVE AMERICANS

California was among the last borderlands settled by the Spanish. To pay back settlers for their work, Spain established the **encomienda system.** It gave settlers the right to tax Native Americans and make them work. Most of the workers were treated as slaves and forced to work on **plantations** in New Spain. Many Native Americans died of disease and exhaustion. The priest **Bartolomé de Las Casas** spoke out against the terrible treatment of Native Americans.

> **Why might de Las Casas have spoken out against the encomienda system?**
>
> _____
>
> _____

CHALLENGE ACTIVITY

Critical Thinking: Identifying Cause and Effect

Make a chart showing the causes and effects of Spain's conquests in the Americas.

Bartolomé de Las Casas	conquistadors	encomienda system
Francisco Pizarro	Hernán Cortés	Malintzin
Moctezuma II	plantations	Juan Ponce de León

DIRECTIONS Answer each question by writing a sentence that contains at least one word from the word bank.

1. Which priest wanted to convert Native Americans to Christianity?

_____

_____

2. What were the farms the Spanish operated in the Americas called?

_____

_____

3. What Spanish system gave settlers the right to tax local Native Americans?

_____

_____

4. Which conquistador defeated the Inca and how did he do it?

_____

_____

5. Who was the king of the Aztec empire when the conquistadors arrived in Mexico?

_____

_____

6. Who was the conquistador that conquered the Aztec empire and who helped him?

_____

_____

7. What were the Spanish soldiers who conquered the Americas called?

_____

_____

New Empires in the Americas

Section 4

MAIN IDEAS
1. Events in Europe affected settlement of North America.
2. Several explorers searched for a Northwest Passage to the Pacific Ocean.
3. European nations raced to establish empires in North America.

Key Terms and People

Protestant Reformation a religious movement that began as an effort to reform the Catholic Church

Protestants the reformers who protested the Catholic Church's practices

Spanish Armada the Spanish fleet of huge warships

Northwest Passage a path through North America that would allow ships to sail from the Atlantic to the Pacific

Jacques Cartier French explorer who sailed up the Saint Lawrence River looking for the Northwest Passage

charter a document giving permission to start a colony

Section Summary

EVENTS IN EUROPE

In 1517 a priest named Martin Luther launched the **Protestant Reformation**. His followers were called **Protestants**. Luther said the Catholic Church was too rich and abused its powers. The printing press helped spread Protestant ideas because large numbers of Bibles could be printed. More people could read the Bible on their own instead of depending on priests to explain it.

Often conflicts between Catholics and Protestants led to war. In the late 1500s French Catholics fought French Protestants known as Huguenots. Many Huguenots traveled to the Americas for religious freedom. In 1534 King Henry VIII established the Church of England, or Anglican Church. Henry declared himself head of this Protestant church. By breaking with the Catholic church, King Henry made himself the enemy of other European rulers who were Catholics.

> How did the printing press help spread Protestant ideas?
>
> _____
>
> _____

> What were French Protestants called?
>
> _____
>
> _____

King Philip II of Spain, a Catholic ruler, put
together a large fleet called the **Spanish Armada** to
defeat the Protestant nation of England. England had
fewer ships, but they were quick. In July 1588 the
English navy defeated the Armada. The defeat hurt
the Spanish, whose economy was in trouble because
of inflation. Inflation is a rise in prices caused by an
increase in the amount of money in use.

What helped England's navy defeat the Spanish Armada?
_____
_____

SEARCH FOR A NORTHWEST PASSAGE

European nations wanted to find a **Northwest
Passage** in North America that would allow ships to
sail from the Atlantic to the Pacific. Early searches
explored the coast from Canada to North Carolina.
Jacques Cartier explored the Saint Lawrence River
and claimed lands for France. The Northwest
Passage was not found, but the voyages led to more
interest in North America.

EUROPEAN PRESENCE IN NORTH AMERICA

Spain and Portugal claimed much of South and
Central America but left most of North America
unexplored. In the late 1500s Sir Walter Raleigh of
England received a **charter** to found a colony in
present-day Virginia. The first colonists did not
stay, but Raleigh sent more colonists. Those
colonists disappeared.

France built settlements in Florida, but the Spanish
soon drove them out. In the 1600s French colonies
were established on the Saint Lawrence River. The
French claimed lands extending to the Mississippi
River. The Dutch founded the town of New
Amsterdam on Manhattan Island. Swedish settlers
started New Sweden along the Delaware River, but it
was conquered by the Dutch colonists in 1655.

What happened to French settlers in Florida?
_____
_____

CHALLENGE ACTIVITY

Critical Thinking: Summarizing Write a bulleted
list summarizing the early settlements of the
Americas.

DIRECTIONS Write two adjectives or descriptive phrases that describe
the term, person, or event.

1. charter _____

2. Jacques Cartier _____

3. Northwest Passage _____

4. Protestant Reformation _____

5. Protestants _____

6. Spanish Armada _____

DIRECTIONS Read each sentence and fill in the blank with the word
in the word pair that best completes the sentence.

7. _____, a French sailor, led a major French exploration
   of what is now Canada in 1534 and 1535. (Jacques Cartier/Henry Hudson)

8. The _____ were reformers who protested some of the
   Catholic Church's practices. (Spanish Armada/Protestants)

9. A _____ is a document giving permission to start a colony.
   (Reformation/charter)

10. Europeans wanted to find a _____, a water route
    through North America that would provide a shortcut to Asia.
    (Northwest Passage/Spanish Armada)

New Empires in the Americas

 MAIN IDEAS
1. European diseases wiped out much of the Native American population, causing colonists to look for a new labor force.
2. Europeans enslaved millions of Africans and sent them to work in their colonies.
3. Slaves in the Americas created a distinct culture.

Key Terms and People

immune having a natural resistance to a disease

Middle Passage the voyage across the Atlantic that enslaved Africans were forced to endure

African Diaspora the scattering of African people due to slavery

Academic Vocabulary

structure the way something is organized

Section Summary

THE NEED FOR A NEW LABOR FORCE

Diseases like measles, smallpox, and typhus had afflicted Europeans for many centuries before they came to the New World. As a result, Europeans were more **immune** to the diseases than Native Americans who had never been exposed to them at all. Therefore, these European diseases had a devastating effect on the Native American population. Millions died in the years after Columbus reached the New World.

Now the European colonists needed a new workforce for their plantations. Plantations were important to the colonial economic **structure**. As Africans had already developed some immunity to European diseases, the colonists decided that slaves from West Africa could be the solution to the labor problem.

> How did the lack of immunity to disease affect the Native American peoples?
>
> _____
>
> _____

> What factors caused colonists to decide to use African slaves?
>
> _____
>
> _____

THE SLAVE TRADE

In 1510 the Spanish government legalized the sale of slaves in its colonies. Over the next century, more than a million African slaves were brought to the Spanish and Portugese colonies. The English and Dutch were also active slave traders.

Enslaved people were often captured in the interior of Africa, chained, and forced to march up to 1,000 miles to the coast. They were then chained together and packed as cargo in the lower decks of ships crossing the Atlantic Ocean. This voyage was known as the **Middle Passage.** In the crowded ships, disease spread quickly. Many of the slaves died of sickness, suffocation, or malnutrition during the voyage.

Between the 1520s and the 1860s, about 12 million Africans were shipped across the Atlantic as slaves. The slave trade led to the **African Diaspora.** Slaves had few rights in the colonies and were considered to be property. The treatment of enslaved Africans varied, but severe treatment and dreadful punishments were often part of American slavery.

> How many people were shipped from Africa as part of the slave trade?
>
> _____
>
> _____

SLAVE CULTURE IN THE AMERICAS

Slaves in America came from many parts of Africa. They spoke different languages and had different cultural backgrounds, but they also shared many customs and viewpoints. They built a new culture on the things they had in common.

Families were a key part of slave culture, but slave families faced many challenges. A family was often broken apart when members were sold to different owners. Religion was a refuge for slaves. Slave religion was primarily Christian, but it also included traditional elements from African religions. Religion gave slaves a sense of self worth and hope for salvation. Slaves used songs and folktales to tell stories of sorrow, hope, agony, and joy.

> Underline the sentence that describes the kind of religion that was common among slaves in the Americas.

CHALLENGE ACTIVITY

Critical Thinking: Elaborate Write a song or folktale that reflects the experiences of enslaved Africans. Your song or folktale should reflect the feelings of sorrow, hope, agony and joy that were included in the songs and folktales of slaves.

DIRECTIONS Read each sentence and fill in the blank with the word
in the word pair that best completes the sentence.

1. Enslaved Africans were forced to endure the _____, which
took them across the Atlantic Ocean to the Americas.
(Middle Passage/plantation agriculture)

2. The slave trade led to the _____, or the scattering of
enslaved Africans all across the New World. (Middle Passage/African Diaspora)

3. Most adult Europeans were _____, or had a natural
resistance, to common diseases in Europe like measles, smallpox, and typhus.
(enslaved/immune)

4. Plantation agriculture was a mainstay of the colonial economic

_____. (structure/property)

DIRECTIONS On the line provided before each statement, write **T** if a
statement is true or **F** if a statement is false. If the statement is false,
find a word or phrase in the word bank that makes the statement true.
Write the new sentence on the line provided.

African Diaspora	immune	Middle Passage

_____ 5. Native Americans had never been exposed to diseases like measles and
smallpox, and they were therefore not <u>Middle Passage</u> to them.

_____

_____

_____ 6. The <u>African Diaspora</u> was the voyage across the Atlantic Ocean in which
slaves were chained together and crammed into spaces about the size of
coffins.

_____

_____

The English Colonies

 MAIN IDEAS
1. The settlement in Jamestown was the first permanent English settlement in America.
2. Daily life in Virginia was challenging to the colonists.
3. Religious freedom and economic opportunities were motives for founding other southern colonies, including Maryland, the Carolinas, and Georgia.
4. Farming and slavery were important to the economies of the southern colonies.

Key Terms and People

Jamestown an English settlement in Virginia founded in 1607

John Smith a colonist and leader of Jamestown

Pocahontas a Powhatan Indian who married Jamestown colonist John Rolfe

indentured servants colonists who reached America by working for free for other people who had paid for their journeys

Bacon's Rebellion an uprising led by Nathaniel Bacon against high taxes

Toleration Act of 1649 an act that made limiting the religious rights of Christians a crime

Olaudah Equiano a former slave who wrote down his experiences

slave codes laws to control slaves

Academic Vocabulary

authority power, right to rule

factors causes

Section Summary

SETTLEMENT IN JAMESTOWN

Life in **Jamestown** was hard. Few colonists knew how to grow crops for food. Captain **John Smith** worried about this. Many colonists starved. The Powhatan helped the colonists learn to grow crops.

Pocahontas helped unite the Powhatan and the colonists, but she died in 1617. Fighting broke out between the colonists and the Powhatan and went on for the next 20 years. The colony existed under the **authority** of a governor chosen by the king.

> **Why did many colonists in Jamestown starve?**
> _____
> _____

DAILY LIFE IN VIRGINIA

Colonists began forming large farms called plantations. At first **indentured servants** worked on plantations. In 1619 the first Africans came to Virginia. These **factors** led wealthy farmers to begin using slave labor.

In 1676 Nathaniel Bacon, a wealthy frontier farmer, led **Bacon's Rebellion**. Bacon and his followers burned Jamestown.

> **What happened to Jamestown in 1676?**
> _____
> _____

OTHER SOUTHERN COLONIES

Maryland was founded south of Virginia as a new colony for Catholics. In the 1640s Protestants began moving in. Religious problems divided Protestants and Catholics. The **Toleration Act of 1649** made limiting religious rights of Christians a crime in Maryland.

The Carolinas and Georgia were formed south of Virginia and Maryland. South Carolina had many large plantations, and owners bought slaves to work on them. In Georgia many huge rice plantations were worked by thousands of slaves.

> **Circle the sentence that explains what the Toleration Act of 1649 did.**

ECONOMIES OF THE SOUTHERN COLONIES

The economies of the southern colonies were based on farming. Many small farms and some small plantations meant a large group of workers was needed. African slaves became these workers. Slavery was brutal. A former slave named **Olaudah Equiano** wrote that slaves were often tortured, murdered, and treated with barbarity. Most of the southern states passed **slave codes** to control slaves.

> **How did a former slave describe treatment of slaves?**
> _____
> _____

CHALLENGE ACTIVITY

Critical Thinking: Designing Design a time line showing the dates of important events in the colonies.

Bacon's Rebellion	Jamestown	Olaudah Equiano
indentured servants	John Smith	Pocahontas
Toleration Act of 1649		

DIRECTIONS Read each sentence and choose the correct term from
the word bank to replace the underlined term. Write the underlined term
in the space provided and then define the term in your own words.

1. John Rolfe wrote about the brutal conditions he experienced as a slave. _____

   Your definition: _____

   _____

   _____

2. Colonists called American Indians signed contracts agreeing to work on
   plantations and farms in exchange for the payment of their journey to America.

   _____

   Your definition: _____

   _____

   _____

3. A group of former indentured servants led by a wealthy frontier farmer began an
   uprising called the Mayflower Compact. _____

   Your definition: _____

   _____

   _____

4. The headright system made restricting religious rights of Christians a crime, and
   was the first law supporting religious tolerance passed in the English colonies.

   _____

   Your definition: _____

   _____

   _____

Guided Reading Workbook

The English Colonies

MAIN IDEAS
1. The Pilgrims and Puritans came to America to avoid religious persecution.
2. Religion and government were closely linked in the New England colonies.
3. The New England economy was based on trade and farming.
4. Education was important in the New England colonies.

Key Terms and People

Puritans a Protestant group that wanted to reform, or purify, the Church of England

Pilgrims a Protestant group that cut all ties with the Church of England and was punished

immigrants people who have left the country of their birth to live in another country

Mayflower Compact a legal contract male passengers on the Mayflower signed agreeing to have fair laws to protect the general good

Squanto a Patuxet Indian who had lived in Europe and spoke English

John Winthrop the leader of Puritans who left England for Massachusetts seeking religious freedom

Anne Hutchinson a Puritan who claimed to receive her religious views directly from God and who was forced to leave the Massachusetts Bay Colony

Section Summary
PILGRIMS AND PURITANS

The **Pilgrims** were a group of **Puritans** who suffered persecution in England. They became **immigrants**, first settling in the Netherlands and then sailing to America.

When they reached America, the Pilgrims signed the **Mayflower Compact**. This was one of the first times English colonists tried to govern themselves. Earlier, in 1215, English nobles had forced the king to give them some rights in Magna Carta. Later the English Bill of Rights provided more liberties.

> **Name two early examples of the English receiving rights.**
>
> _____
>
> _____

The Pilgrims learned to fertilize their soil from **Squanto**. They invited him and 90 Wampanoag guests to a feast now known as Thanksgiving.

Religion and education played important parts in the Pilgrims' lives, which centered on families. Everyone worked hard. Women had rights that they did not have in England.

Puritans and merchants founded the Massachusetts Bay colony. Tens of thousands of English men, women and children would immigrate to it. **John Winthrop** led one group. Puritans believed they had a sacred agreement with God to build a Christian colony.

> **What was the Puritans' sacred agreement with God?**
>
> _____
>
> _____

RELIGION AND GOVERNMENT IN NEW ENGLAND

Politics and religion were closely linked in Puritan New England. Some self-government existed. However, only the chosen male church members could vote.

Some Puritans had different religious views than others. Minister Roger Williams supported the separation of the church from politics. He founded Providence. **Anne Hutchinson** was forced to leave the colony because of her religious ideas.

> **Underline the sentence that means women could not vote in Puritan New England.**

NEW ENGLAND ECONOMY

The New England colonies had a hard climate and rocky soil. The kind of farming done in Virginia was impossible there. Instead, they traded goods, fished, built ships, and became skilled craftspeople.

> **Compare sources of income in Virginia and New England.**
>
> _____
>
> _____

EDUCATION IN THE COLONIES

New England parents wanted their children to read the Bible. They made laws requiring the education of children. The colonists also founded Harvard College to teach ministers.

CHALLENGE ACTIVITY

Critical Thinking: Developing Questions

Develop three questions about the Pilgrims' contributions and research to answer them.

Anne Hutchinson	John Winthrop	Pilgrims
immigrants	Mayflower Compact	Puritans
Squanto		

DIRECTIONS Answer each question by writing a sentence that contains at least one word from the word bank.

1. Who was put on trial for his or her religious ideas and eventually forced out of the colony?

   _____

   _____

2. Who are people that leave their country of birth to live in another country?

   _____

   _____

3. Who showed the Pilgrims how to fertilize the soil on their farms and helped them establish relations with the chief of the local Wampanoag Indians?

   _____

   _____

4. Who led a group of Puritan colonists who left England for Massachusetts in search of religious freedom?

   _____

   _____

5. What Protestant group wanted to reform, or purify, the Church of England?

   _____

   _____

DIRECTIONS Choose at least five of the vocabulary words from the word bank. On a separate sheet of paper, use these words to write a letter that relates to the section.

The English Colonies

MAIN IDEAS
1. The English created New York and New Jersey from former Dutch territory.
2. William Penn established the colony of Pennsylvania.
3. The economy of the middle colonies was supported by trade and staple crops.

Key Terms and People

Peter Stuyvesant director general who took control of New Amsterdam beginning in 1647

Quakers a Protestant religious group founded by George Fox in the mid-1600s in England

William Penn a Quaker leader who began the Pennsylvania colony

staple crops crops that are always needed, such as wheat, barley, and oats

Section Summary

NEW YORK AND NEW JERSEY

In 1613 the Dutch formed New Netherland as a base for trading fur with the Iroquois. They traded fur mostly in the town of New Amsterdam on Manhattan Island. Large land grants and religious tolerance meant Jews, French Huguenots, Puritans, and others came to the colony.

Peter Stuyvesant ruled the colony for many years. Then in 1664 an English fleet gained control of New Netherland without any fighting. New Amsterdam became New York City, named in honor of the Duke of York. New York was the first of the middle colonies.

The Duke of York made two men proprietors, or governors, of New Jersey. The colony rested between the Hudson and Delaware Rivers. Dutch, Finns, Swedes, Scots, and others lived there.

PENN'S COLONY

One of the biggest religious groups in New Jersey was the Society of Friends, or the Quakers. Their religious practices were different. They believed in

> What was the first town on Manhattan Island?
>
> _____
> _____

> Why did the Dutch settle New Amsterdam?
>
> _____
> _____

> Underline the sentence that makes you think the population of New Jersey was diverse.

the equality of men and women before God. They also backed religious tolerance for all groups. The Quakers' beliefs angered many. They were treated badly in both England and America.

William Penn started a colony named Pennsylvania. He offered religious freedom to all Christians. He created a way to change colony laws based on what the people wanted. Many Quakers settled in Pennsylvania. Penn named his capital Philadelphia, which means "the city of Brotherly Love."

> **What does Philadelphia mean?**
> _____
> _____

ECONOMY OF THE MIDDLE COLONIES

A good climate and fertile land meant the colonists could grow a large quantity of **staple crops**, unlike colonists in New England. Some slaves worked in the middle colonies but not as many as in the south. Indentured servants did more of the labor.

> **How did the middle and southern colonies differ?**
> _____
> _____

By the 1700s Philadelphia and New York City had grown into large cities. Trade was important to the middle colonies. Women ran some businesses and practiced as doctors, nurses, or midwives.

CHALLENGE ACTIVITY

Critical Thinking: Evaluating Think about the Middle colonies. How are they similar? How are they different? Decide which colony you would like to live in. Then write a short essay explaining why you chose the colony you did. Illustrate your essay.

| Peter Stuyvesant | staple crops | Quakers | William Penn |

DIRECTIONS Use all the vocabulary words from the word bank to write a summary of what you learned in this section.

_____

_____

_____

_____

_____

_____

_____

DIRECTIONS Read each sentence and fill in the blank with the word in the word pair that best completes the sentence.

1. Director General _____ controlled the colony of New Amsterdam beginning in 1647. (John Rolfe/Peter Stuyvesant)

2. _____ are items that are always needed, such as wheat and barley. (Staple crops/Cash crops)

3. The _____ supported the equality of men and women before God, religious tolerance, and nonviolence. (Dutch/Quakers)

4. Pennsylvania was established by _____ to provide a government that was fair to all people. (William Penn/John Winthrop)

5. The economy of the middle colonies depended on the production of

_____, skilled labor, and trade. (tobacco/staple crops)

The English Colonies

Section 4

MAIN IDEAS
1. Colonial governments were influenced by political changes in England.
2. English trade laws limited free trade in the colonies.
3. The Great Awakening and the Enlightenment led to ideas of political equality among many colonists.
4. The French and Indian War gave England control of more land in North America.

Key Terms and People

town meeting an assembly in which colonists decided issues and made laws

English Bill of Rights an act passed in 1689 that reduced the powers of the English monarch and gave Parliament more power

triangular trade indirect trade between the American colonies and Britain

Jonathan Edwards important leader of the Great Awakening

Great Awakening an awakening in the religious lives of colonists

Enlightenment a movement during the 1700s that focused on the use of reason and logic to improve society

Pontiac Native American leader who led a rebellion in the Ohio Valley in 1763

Section Summary
COLONIAL GOVERNMENTS

The House of Burgesses helped make laws in Virginia. In New England, colonists at **town meeting** decided local issues. The middle colonies used both county courts and town meetings.

King James II of England thought the colonies were too independent. He united the northern colonies and limited their powers. In 1689 the **English Bill of Rights** shifted power from the monarch to Parliament, the British governing body. These rights were not extended to the colonists.

> **How were laws made in Virginia and New England?**
> _____
> _____

> **Did the colonists benefit from the English Bill of Rights?**
> _____

ENGLISH TRADE LAWS

England controlled its American colonies partly to earn money. Parliament passed Navigation Acts that required colonists to trade only with Britain.

Guided Reading Workbook

However, some colonists wanted to buy and sell goods at the market offering the best prices.

In a deadly version of **triangular trade**, New England colonists traded rum for slaves from the African coast. The slave trade forced 10 million Africans across the Atlantic Ocean. In the Middle Passage thousands of them died.

What is the name given to the voyage of slaves from Africa to America?
_____

GREAT AWAKENING AND ENLIGHTENMENT

During the **Great Awakening** talk of spiritual equality made some people, such as **Jonathan Edwards**, think about political equality. **Enlightenment** thinker John Locke said people should obey their rulers only if the state protected life, liberty, and property.

In 1675 a war erupted between New England colonists and some American Indians. Metacomet, who was also known as King Philip, led the Wampanoag. Each side killed men, women, and children. The fighting ended in 1676.

What was King Philip's real name?
_____

THE FRENCH AND INDIAN WAR

The British and the French both wanted to control certain territory in North America. The French and Indian War was about the British wanting to settle in the Ohio Valley and the French wanting it for the fur trade. After the war Britain won Canada and all French lands east of the Mississippi River.

The Ohio Valley proved good for farming, but Native American leaders opposed British settlements. American Indian Chief **Pontiac** led followers against the British. He later gave up, but King George III banned colonists from settling on Indian lands. Many settlers ignored the ban.

How did many Americans react to the king's ban on settling on Indian lands?
_____

CHALLENGE ACTIVITY

Critical Thinking: Drawing Inferences Imagine you live during the Enlightenment. Write a short journal entry describing the time.

DIRECTIONS Look at each set of four terms. On the line provided, write the letter of the term that does not relate to the others.

_____ 1. a. House of Burgesses
        b. town meetings
        c. governors
        d. Great Awakening

_____ 4. a. revivals
        b. Jonathan Edwards
        c. Great Awakening
        d. colonial courts

_____ 2. a. Navigation Acts
        b. English Bill of Rights
        c. mercantilism
        d. free enterprise

_____ 5. a. triangular trade
        b. Proclamation of 1763
        c. French and Indian War
        d. Pontiac's Rebellion

_____ 3. a. slavery
        b. triangular trade
        c. John Winthrop
        d. Middle Passage

DIRECTIONS Write two adjectives or descriptive phrases that describe each term.

6. House of Burgesses _____

7. Jonathan Edwards _____

8. French and Indian War _____

9. English Bill of Rights _____

10. Great Awakening _____

The English Colonies

MAIN IDEAS
1. British efforts to raise taxes on colonists sparked protest.
2. The Boston Massacre caused colonial resentment toward Great Britain.
3. Colonists protested the British tax on tea with the Boston Tea Party.
4. Great Britain responded to colonial actions by passing the Intolerable Acts.

Key Terms and People

Samuel Adams Boston leader who believed Parliament could not tax the colonists without their permission

Committees of Correspondence method of communication between towns and colonies about British laws

Stamp Act of 1765 required colonists to pay for an official stamp when buying paper items

Boston Massacre shooting by British soldiers killed five colonists

Tea Act an act allowing a British company to sell cheap tea directly to the colonists

Boston Tea Party a protest in which colonists dressed as American Indians and dumped 340 tea chests from British ships into Boston Harbor

Intolerable Acts laws passed to punish colonists for the Boston Tea Party

Section Summary

GREAT BRITAIN RAISES TAXES

Parliament raised the colonists' taxes for money to pay for the French and Indian War. The tax money was also used to keep a British army in North America to protect the colonists against American Indian attacks. Parliament also tried harder to arrest smugglers avoiding taxes.

Many colonists believed Britain had no right to tax them without their permission. Colonists communicated their ideas about British laws in **Committees of Correspondence. Samuel Adams** and James Otis spread the slogan "No Taxation without Representation." Colonists chose to boycott, refusing to buy British goods. They hoped Parliament would end the new taxes. The **Stamp**

> **Name one reason that Parliament raised taxes.**
> _____
> _____

> **How did colonists respond to British taxes?**
> _____
> _____

Act of 1765 meant a tax had to be paid on legal documents, licenses, and other items.

The Townshend Acts charged taxes on imported glass, lead, paints, paper, and tea. Boston's Sons of Liberty attacked the customs houses to protest the taking of a ship on suspicion of smuggling. British soldiers came in 1768 to restore order.

> Underline the sentence that tells what the Townshend Acts did.

BOSTON MASSACRE

On March 5, 1770, a few troops fired on Bostonians who were throwing snowballs at them. That led to the **Boston Massacre**. The soldiers and their officer were charged with murder. A jury found the officer and six soldiers acted in self-defense and were not guilty. Two soldiers were convicted of accidental killing. This calmed Boston for a while.

> Why do you think the jury found some of the troops not guilty?
> _____
> _____
> _____

THE BOSTON TEA PARTY

Parliament ended almost all the Townshend Acts but left the tax on tea. Colonists united against the **Tea Act**. In November 1773 the **Boston Tea Party** showed the colonists' spirit of rebellion.

THE INTOLERABLE ACTS

The Boston Tea Party made the new British Prime Minister very angry. Parliament punished Boston by passing the **Intolerable Acts**. The laws closed Boston Harbor until the colonists paid for the lost tea. Other parts of the Intolerable Acts angered the colonists even more.

> Why did the Boston Tea Party anger the British Prime Minister?
> _____
> _____
> _____

CHALLENGE ACTIVITY

Critical Thinking: Imagining Imagine you write for Boston's Committee of Correspondence. Give a brief description of the Boston Massacre.

DIRECTIONS Match the definition with the correct term from the right column.

_____ 1. These groups were created to share information with other towns and colonies about ways to challenge British laws.

_____ 2. In this event, colonists disguised as American Indians dumped more than 340 tea chests into Boston Harbor.

_____ 3. These laws were designed to punish the colonists in Boston for their actions against the British.

_____ 4. This man wrote and circulated papers encouraging colonists to join the protest against unfair taxation.

_____ 5. This took place when British soldiers fired into a crowd, killing five colonists.

a. Boston Massacre

b. Boston Tea Party

c. Committees of Correspondence

d. Intolerable Acts

e. Samuel Adams

DIRECTIONS Read each sentence and fill in the blank with the word that best completes the sentence.

6. Samuel Adams helped found the _____, which shared ideas and information about the new British laws and ways to challenge them. (House of Burgesses/Committees of Correspondence)

7. The _____ required colonists to pay for an official stamp, or seal, whenever they bought paper items. (Townshend Acts/Stamp Act)

8. As part of the _____, Boston Harbor was closed until colonists paid for tea destroyed in the Boston Tea Party. (Intolerable Acts/Tea Act)

9. The _____ was used as propaganda against the British by Samuel Adams and other protestors. (Boston Massacre/Boston Tea Party)

10. _____ helped create the Sons of Liberty to protest and use violence to frighten tax collectors. (Samuel Adams/George Grenville)

The American Revolution

 MAIN IDEAS

1. The First Continental Congress demanded certain rights from Great Britain.
2. Armed conflict between British soldiers and colonists broke out with the "shot heard 'round the world."
3. The Second Continental Congress created the Continental Army to fight the British.
4. In two early battles, the army lost control of Boston but then regained it.

Key Terms and People

First Continental Congress gathering of colonial leaders who were deeply troubled about the relationship between Great Britain and its colonies in America

Patriots colonists who chose to fight for independence

minutemen the members of the civilian volunteer militia

Redcoats British soldiers wearing red uniforms

Second Continental Congress meeting of delegates from 12 colonies in Philadelphia in May 1775

Continental Army army created by the Second Continental Congress to carry out the fight against Britain

George Washington the Virginian who commanded the Continental Army

Battle of Bunker Hill battle won by the British but with double the American losses

Academic Vocabulary

reaction response

Section Summary
FIRST CONTINENTAL CONGRESS

Delegates to the **First Continental Congress** were worried about the relationship between Great Britain and its American colonies. The delegates debated whether violence was avoidable. They encouraged the peaceful boycott of British goods but also began preparing for war. They drafted a Declaration of Rights, but King George refused to consider it. Colonists who chose to fight for independence were known as **Patriots**.

> **What did the delegates debate?**
>
> _____
>
> _____

"SHOT HEARD 'ROUND THE WORLD"

On April 19, 1775, 700 **Redcoats** set out for Concord. A British general sent the soldiers to destroy a weapons storehouse they thought was there. Three colonists rode out on horseback to warn that the British were coming. Seventy armed **minutemen** waited for the British at Lexington. To this day nobody knows who fired the first shot. The British killed eight minutemen, then went on to Concord where they destroyed a few buildings. In **reaction** the minutemen fired on the Redcoats. The British suffered many casualties and were forced to retreat.

> **Why did the British soldiers go to Concord?**
> _____
> _____

SECOND CONTINENTAL CONGRESS

At the **Second Continental Congress** some delegates called for war while others wanted peace. The Congress named the Massachusetts militia the **Continental Army**. The army's commander was **George Washington**. Delegates signed the Olive Branch Petition asking King George to make peace. He would not consider it.

> **What was King George's response to the Olive Branch Petition?**
> _____
> _____

EARLY BATTLES

On June 17, 1775, the British in Boston found colonial forces dug in on Breed's Hill. When the British crossed the harbor in boats to take the hill, the colonists opened fire. The British took the hill on their third try. But the **Battle of Bunker Hill** proved the colonists could hold their own. Soon after, General Washington took command of the Continental Army in Boston. He set up cannons from Fort Ticonderoga to fire on the British. On March 7, 1776, the British retreated from Boston.

CHALLENGE ACTIVITY

Critical Thinking: Analyze List several rights we have as U.S. citizens.

DIRECTIONS Read each sentence and fill in the blank with the word
in the word pair that best completes the sentence.

1. The _____ chose not to break away from Britain but did
   create a military force and a new currency with which to pay the soldiers.
   (First Continental Congress/Second Continental Congress)

2. General George Washington led the main colonial military force, which was

   called the _____. (Continental Army/minutemen)

3. All of the colonies except Georgia sent delegates to the _____
   to discuss Great Britain's decision to close the port of Boston.
   (First Continental Congress/Second Continental Congress)

4. Members of the civilian volunteer militia of Massachusetts were known as

   _____. (minutemen/Redcoats)

5. Although the colonists lost, the _____ proved that they
   could take on the British. (Battle of Bunker Hill/Seige of Fort Ticonderoga)

DIRECTIONS Write two adjectives or descriptive phrases that describe
the term, person, or event.

6. Battle of Bunker Hill _____

7. George Washington _____

8. minutemen _____

9. Redcoats _____

10. Second Continental Congress _____

The American Revolution

MAIN IDEAS
1. Thomas Paine's *Common Sense* led many colonists to support independence.
2. Colonists had to choose sides when independence was declared.
3. The Declaration of Independence did not address the rights of all colonists.

Key Terms and People

Common Sense a 47-page pamphlet that argued against British rule over America

Thomas Paine author of *Common Sense*, who wrote that citizens, not monarchs, should make laws

Thomas Jefferson the main author of the Declaration of Independence

Declaration of Independence the document that formally announced the colonies' break from Great Britain

Loyalists colonists, sometimes called Tories, who remained loyal to Britain

Section Summary

PAINE'S *COMMON SENSE*

Common Sense was published anonymously, or without the name of its author, who was **Thomas Paine**. At this time the idea that citizens should pass laws made news. As word of the pamphlet spread throughout the colonies, it eventually sold about 500,000 copies. The pamphlet made a strong case for political and economic freedom. It supported the right to military self-defense. *Common Sense* changed the way many colonists viewed their king.

Why do you think *Common Sense* was so popular?
_____
_____

INDEPENDENCE IS DECLARED

The first point argued by **Thomas Jefferson** in the **Declaration of Independence** was that all men possess unalienable rights, or rights that cannot be denied. These rights include "life, liberty, and the pursuit of happiness." Jefferson also maintained that King George III had trampled on the colonists' rights by supporting unfair laws and wrongly

Guided Reading Workbook

meddling in colonial governments. In addition
Jefferson argued that the colonies had the right to
independence from Britain. He believed in the
Enlightenment idea of the social contract. This idea
says that citizens should agree to be governed only
when rulers and governments support their rights.
Jefferson said that King George III had violated the
social contract, so the colonies should not obey his
laws.

> **Why did Jefferson think the colonies should not obey King George III?**
> _____
> _____

On July 4, 1776, the Continental Congress voted
in favor of the Declaration of Independence. In
approving the Declaration, the Congress finally
broke away from Great Britain. Today we celebrate
the Fourth of July as the birthday of our nation.

Not everyone rejoiced over the approval of the
Declaration. Patriots and **Loyalists** became divided.
Sometimes family members were on opposite sides
during the war. More than 50,000 Loyalists left the
colonies during the Revolution.

> **What did some families experience during the war?**
> _____
> _____

UNFINISHED BUSINESS

Looking back, we realize that the Declaration paid
no attention to many colonists. Abigail Adams, wife
of delegate John Adams, tried to influence him to
include women in the Declaration. It did not
happen. Enslaved African Americans also had no
rights under the Declaration. Slavery was legal in
all colonies in July 1776. The Revolutionary War
would not end the battle over slavery, even though
New England states moved to end it by the 1780s.

> **Name two groups who had no rights under the Declaration.**
> _____
> _____

CHALLENGE ACTIVITY

Critical Thinking: Develop Imagine that you are a
delegate to the Second Continental Congress.
Deliver a two-minute speech arguing that the
Declaration should also give women and slaves
rights.

Common Sense	Thomas Jefferson	Loyalists
Patriots	unalienable	Thomas Paine
Tyranny	Declaration of Independence	

DIRECTIONS Answer each question by writing a sentence that contains at least one word from the word bank.

1. What did Thomas Paine write to encourage the colonists to declare independence?

_____

_____

2. What did the Second Continental Congress do to formally declare the colonies free from Great Britain?

_____

_____

3. What group of colonists faced hostility as a result of their views regarding the Declaration of Independence?

_____

_____

4. Who was the main author of the Declaration of Independence, and what three main points did he make in the document?

_____

_____

_____

_____

_____

The American Revolution

MAIN IDEAS
1. Many Americans supported the war effort.
2. The Patriots both won and lost battles during the years 1775–1777.
3. France and Spain helped the Patriots fight the British.
4. The winter at Valley Forge tested the strength of Patriot troops.
5. The war continued at sea and in the West.

Key Terms and People

mercenaries foreign soldiers who fought not out of loyalty, but for pay

Battle of Trenton a battle won by the Patriots against mercenary Hessians

Battle of Saratoga a great victory for the American forces in which British General John Burgoyne surrendered his entire army to American General Horatio Gates

Marquis de Lafayette a Frenchman who volunteered to serve in the Continental Army without pay and used his money and influence to support the Patriots

Baron Friedrich von Steuben a Prussian military officer who trained the Continental Army

Bernardo de Gálvez the governor of Spanish Louisiana, who became a Patriot ally

John Paul Jones a brave and clever naval commander

George Rogers Clark a surveyor who led the Patriots' western campaign

Academic Vocabulary

strategy a plan for fighting a battle or war

Section Summary

SUPPORTING THE WAR EFFORT

Life in the army was hard, but the Patriots knew they were fighting for an important cause. More than 230,000 mostly young men served in the Continental Army. After the British promised to free any slaves who fought for them, the Continental Army allowed free African Americans to serve. Women played an important role in the war by helping to supply the army and serving as messengers, nurses, and spies.

> Underline the sentence that tells how some women served the war effort.

DEFEATS AND VICTORIES

At first the Continental Army lost several battles. Then the Patriots won an important victory. British General Howe, who thought the rebellion would soon be over, left New Jersey in the hands of Hessian **mercenaries**. The Patriots surprised the Hessians and won the **Battle of Trenton**.

British General John Burgoyne planned to cut off New England from the other colonies. His **strategy** required perfect timing. The Patriots surrounded Burgoyne and won the **Battle of Saratoga**, which was the turning point of the war.

> Circle the name of an early victory for the Patriots.

HELP FROM EUROPE

Britain's enemies, France and Spain, began to help the Patriots. Holland also helped the Patriots. The **Marquis de Lafayette, Baron Friedrich von Steuben,** and **Bernardo de Gálvez** joined the war on the Patriots' side.

WINTER AT VALLEY FORGE

The winter of 1777 turned brutally cold and snowy. General Washington settled his troops at Valley Forge, where they bore hardships with courage and drilled to become better soldiers.

WAR AT SEA AND IN THE WEST

The small Continental Navy sunk hundreds of British ships. **John Paul Jones** fought a battle with the British in which his ship took heavy damage. He fought on, and the British ship surrendered. In the West, **George Rogers Clark** led Patriots against British trading villages and Fort Sackville. Clark's campaigns hurt British support in the West.

> What effect did Clark's campaigns have on the British?
>
> _____
>
> _____

CHALLENGE ACTIVITY

Critical Thinking: Elaborate Write and perform a dialogue between two soldiers discussing their hard times at Valley Forge.

Battle of Saratoga	Battle of Trenton	Bernardo de Gálvez
George Rogers Clark	Horatio Gates	John Paul Jones
mercenaries	Marquis de Lafayette	

DIRECTIONS Read each sentence and choose the correct term from the word bank to replace the underlined phrase. Write the term in the space provided and then define the term in your own words.

1. In <u>this battle</u>, the Patriots crossed the Delaware River on Christmas night, 1776, in a successful surprise attack on Hessian mercenaries. _____

    Your definition: _____

    _____

2. The Patriot victory at <u>this battle in New York</u> was an important turning point in the war. _____

    Your definition: _____

    _____

3. <u>This French nobleman</u> served in the Continental Army and became a skilled military officer. _____

    Your definition: _____

    _____

4. <u>This Patriot sailor</u> gained fame when he captured the British warship *Serapis* in 1779. _____

    Your definition: _____

    _____

The American Revolution

MAIN IDEAS
1. Patriot forces faced many problems in the war in the South.
2. The American Patriots finally defeated the British at the Battle of Yorktown.
3. The British and the Americans officially ended the war by signing the Treaty of Paris of 1783.

Key Terms and People

Francis Marion a Patriot leader who used hit-and-run attacks, known as guerilla warfare

Comte de Rochambeau commander of 4,000 French troops that aided the Patriot forces at the Battle of Yorktown

Battle of Yorktown the last major battle of the American Revolution

Treaty of Paris of 1783 the peace agreement in which Great Britain recognized the independence of the United States

Section Summary
WAR IN THE SOUTH

The war in the northern colonies did not go as the British government had hoped. The northern Patriots were tough to beat. The British moved the war into the South, where they believed large groups of Loyalists would help them win. General Henry Clinton led the British troops. The British plan worked at first.

The war in the South proved especially nasty. Patriots and Loyalists engaged in direct fighting. The British wiped out crops, farm animals, and property. Georgia fell to the British. Next, the British conquered the port of Charleston, South Carolina. The Patriots failed to retake Camden, South Carolina.

Patriot General Nathanael Greene arrived to shape up the army. Meanwhile, under the leadership of **Francis Marion**, the Southern patriots used surprise attacks to cut off British communication

> Why did the British move the war to the South?
> _____
> _____

> Underline the sentence that explains how the British army waged war in the South.

> How did Francis Marion and his men hurt the British?
> _____
> _____

and supply lines. The British could not capture Marion and his men.

BATTLE OF YORKTOWN

The Patriots were in trouble in early 1781. They had little money for paying soldiers and buying supplies. The British held most of the South as well as Philadelphia and New York.

The Continental Army began to pressure the British in the Carolinas. General Charles Cornwallis moved his 7,200 men to Yorktown, Virginia. In New York, General Washington combined his troops with French troops commanded by **Comte de Rochambeau**. Washington marched his force to Virginia in hopes of trapping Cornwallis in Yorktown.

With 16,000 soldiers, Washington's force surrounded Cornwallis. For weeks the French-American force wore down the British troops. Finally, the British surrendered. The Patriots captured 8,000 British prisoners at the **Battle of Yorktown**.

What was Cornwallis's mistake in battle strategy?
_____
_____

THE TREATY OF PARIS

Britain lost most of its army at Yorktown and could not afford a new one. So Great Britain and America began peace talks. Delegates took more than two years to reach a peace agreement.

The Treaty of Paris of 1783 gave the United States independence from Great Britain. It also created America's borders. In a separate treaty, Britain returned Florida to the Spanish. The Patriots' courage had won the Revolutionary War.

Why might reaching a peace treaty have taken so long?
_____
_____

CHALLENGE ACTIVITY

Critical Thinking: Predict Imagine that the Patriots had lost the Revolutionary War. Help lead a class discussion on how your lives would be different today.

| Battle of Yorktown | Comte de Rochambeau | Francis Marion |
| Horatio Gates | Treaty of Paris of 1783 | Nathanael Greene |

DIRECTIONS Use the vocabulary terms and names from the word list above to write a letter, journal entry, or poem that relates to the section.

_____

_____

_____

_____

_____

_____

_____

_____

DIRECTIONS Look at each set of four vocabulary terms. On the line provided, write the letter of the term that does not relate to the others.

_____ 1. a. Nathanael Greene
      b. Horatio Gates
      c. Francis Marion
      d. Charles Cornwallis

_____ 2. a. Savannah, GA
      b. Charleston, SC
      c. Philadelphia, PA
      d. Yorktown, VA

Forming a Government

 MAIN IDEAS
1. The American people examined many ideas about government.
2. The Articles of Confederation laid the base for the first national government of the United States.
3. The Confederation Congress established the Northwest Territory.

Key Terms and People

Magna Carta an English document that limited the power of the monarch

constitution a set of basic principles and laws that states the powers and duties of the government

Virginia Statute for Religious Freedom a law that included Thomas Jefferson's ideas granting religious freedom

suffrage voting rights

Articles of Confederation the new national constitution, which made a new Confederation Congress the national government

ratification official approval of the Articles of Confederation by the states

Land Ordinance of 1785 a law that set up a system for surveying land and dividing the Northwest Territory

Northwest Ordinance of 1787 a law that established the Northwest Territory and formed a political system for the region

Northwest Territory a territory including Illinois, Indiana, Michigan, Ohio, and Wisconsin

Section Summary

IDEAS ABOUT GOVERNMENT

After winning independence from Great Britain, the United States needed to form new governments. The Americans first looked to English law for ideas. The English Bill of Rights and **Magna Carta** gave them inspiration. Ideas from the Enlightenment also influenced them. English philosopher John Locke had thought the government had a duty to guard people's rights.

> **Where did Americans find ideas for their government?**
>
> _____
>
> _____

In 1639 the people of Connecticut had created a government plan considered to be the first written **constitution** in the colonies. During the American Revolution nearly every state wrote a constitution to ensure that citizens elected representatives to make laws. **Suffrage** varied considerably from state to state. Some constitutions banned slavery. The **Virginia Statute for Religious Freedom** was an example of a law providing religious freedom.

> **Should the states that banned slavery have been more insistent that other states ban it also? Why or why not?**
>
> _____
>
> _____
>
> _____

ARTICLES OF CONFEDERATION

The Continental Congress named a Committee of Thirteen, with one member from each colony. This committee drafted the **Articles of Confederation**.

Under the Articles the Confederation Congress had limited powers to guard the people's freedoms. Each state had one vote in the Congress. The Congress had powers, but it could only ask the states for money and soldiers. States could refuse these requests. After some conflicts the Articles were **ratified** by all the states to form the first American government.

> **Why would you have voted for or against the Articles?**
>
> _____
>
> _____

NORTHWEST TERRITORY

Congress decided to raise money to pay debts by selling the ordinance lands. Congress passed the **Land Ordinance of 1785**. The **Northwest Ordinance of 1787** formed the **Northwest Territory**. It was then split up into several smaller territories. When the population of a territory hit 60,000, its settlers could draft their own constitution and ask to join the Union. Slavery was banned in the Northwest Territory.

> **Underline the sentence that explains when a territory could ask to join the Union.**

CHALLENGE ACTIVITY

Critical Thinking: Elaborating You plan to settle in the Northwest Territory. List 10 items you will take with you and explain why you chose the items you did.

| Constitution | Magna Carta |
| Virginia Statute for Religious Freedom | Articles of Confederation |

DIRECTIONS Read each sentence and choose the correct term from the word bank to replace the underlined phrase. Write the term in the space provided and then define the term in your own words.

1. The <u>Land Ordinance of 1785</u> was the national constitution created by the thirteen-member committee appointed by the Second Continental Congress.

   _____

   Your definition: _____

   _____

2. The <u>English Bill of Rights,</u> which included Jefferson's ideas about religious freedom, stated that no Virginian would be forced to attend a particular church nor to pay for one with tax money. _____

   Your definition: _____

   _____

3. <u>Northwest Territory,</u> which limited the power of England's kings and queens, was signed by King John in 1215. _____

   Your definition: _____

   _____

4. A <u>Virginia Statute for Religious Freedom</u> is a set of basic principles and laws that states the powers and duties of the government. _____

   Your definition: _____

   _____

Forming a Government

MAIN IDEAS
1. The United States had difficulties with other nations.
2. Internal economic problems plagued the new nation.
3. Shays's Rebellion pointed out weaknesses in the Articles of Confederation.
4. Many Americans called for changes in the national government.

Key Terms and People

tariffs taxes on imports or exports

interstate commerce trade between two or more states

inflation increased prices combined with the reduced value of money

depression a period of low economic activity combined with a rise in unemployment

Daniel Shays a poor farmer and Revolutionary War veteran

Shays's Rebellion an uprising in which Daniel Shays led hundreds of men in a forced shutdown of the Supreme Court in Springfield, Massachusetts

Section Summary

RELATIONS WITH OTHER COUNTRIES

The Continental Army broke up soon after the signing of the Treaty of Paris of 1783. The Articles of Confederation provided no way to raise a new army. The United States had a hard time guarding against foreign threats.

Problems arose in trading with Britain, which closed many British ports to U.S. ships. The British also forced American merchants to pay high **tariffs**. U.S. merchants increased prices to pay them, and costs were passed on to customers.

In 1784 Spanish officials shut down the lower Mississippi River to U.S. shipping. Western farmers and merchants used the river to ship goods east and overseas. The U.S. government failed to work out an agreement with Spain. Critics thought Spain would have negotiated longer if America had a strong military force. The loss of the British West Indies markets meant farmers could not sell goods

> **Point out one weakness in the Articles of Confederation.**
> _____
> _____

> **Why did tariffs hurt U.S. citizens?**
> _____
> _____

there. U.S. exports dropped while lower-priced British goods kept entering America. Congress could not pass tariffs.

ECONOMIC PROBLEMS

Trade problems among the states, war debt, and a poor economy hurt the states. The Confederation Congress had no power to regulate **interstate commerce**. States looked out only for their own trade interests.

In addition, states had trouble paying off war debts. They printed paper money, but it had no gold or silver backing and little value. This caused **inflation**, which occurs when increased prices for goods and services combine with the reduced value of money. The loss of trade with Britain coupled with inflation created a **depression**.

> Underline the sentence that lists problems facing the states.

> What conditions caused a depression in the United States?
>
> _____
>
> _____

SHAYS'S REBELLION

Massachusetts collected taxes on land to pay its war debt. This policy hurt farmers who owned land. The courts made them sell their property to pay taxes. **Daniel Shays** and his followers defied a state order that would stop **Shays's Rebellion**. They were defeated by state troops, and 14 leaders were sentenced to death. However, the state freed most, including Shays. Many citizens agreed with Shays.

CALLS FOR CHANGE

The weaknesses of the Confederation government led leaders, including James Madison and Alexander Hamilton, to ask all 13 states to send delegates to a Constitutional Convention. It was held in Philadelphia in May 1787 to revise the Articles of Confederation and create a better constitution.

CHALLENGE ACTIVITY

Critical Thinking: Predicting Consider how the new U.S. Constitution might change the Articles of Confederation. List three key changes.

| Tariffs | interstate commerce | depression |
| Daniel Shays | Shays's Rebellion | inflation |

DIRECTIONS Answer each question by writing a sentence that contains at least one word from the word bank.

1. What happens when there is an increase in prices for good and services combined with a reduction in the value of money?

_____

_____

2. What do we call taxes on imports and exports?

_____

_____

3. What revolt was started by farmers in three western Massachusetts counties?

_____

_____

4. What do we call a period of low economic activity combined with a rise in unemployment?

_____

_____

5. Who was the leader of the group of farmers that forced a shutdown of the Supreme Court in Springfield, Massachusetts, in 1786?

_____

_____

6. What do we call trade between two or more states?

_____

_____

Forming a Government

MAIN IDEAS
1. The Constitutional Convention met to improve the U.S. government.
2. The issue of representation led to the Great Compromise.
3. Regional debate over slavery led to the Three-Fifths Compromise.
4. The U.S. Constitution created federalism and a balance of power.

Key Terms and People

Constitutional Convention meeting held in Philadelphia to create a new constitution

James Madison a leading convention delegate from Virginia

Virginia Plan a plan giving supreme power to the central government and creating a bicameral legislature made of two groups, or houses, of representatives

New Jersey Plan a plan creating a unicameral, or one-house, legislature

Great Compromise an agreement that gave each state one vote in the upper house and a number of representatives based on its population in the lower house

Three-Fifths Compromise only three-fifths of a state's slaves were counted when deciding representation in Congress

popular sovereignty the idea that political power belongs to the people

federalism the sharing of power between a central government and the states

legislative branch a Congress of two houses that proposes and passes laws

executive branch the president and the departments that help run the government

judicial branch a system of all the national courts

checks and balances a system that keeps any branch of government from becoming too powerful

amendments changes or additions to the Constitution

Section Summary
CONSTITUTIONAL CONVENTION

The **Constitutional Convention** met in May 1787 in Philadelphia, where America had declared independence. Twelve states sent delegates. Most delegates were educated and had served in state legislatures or Congress. **James Madison** attended.

> Name one reason Philadelphia was chosen as the site of the Convention.
>
> _____
> _____

GREAT COMPROMISE

States disagreed about representation, tariffs, slavery, and strength of the central government. In the **Virginia Plan**, the legislature would be selected on the basis of population. The **New Jersey Plan** proposed that each state receive an equal number of votes. The **Great Compromise** gave every state, regardless of size, an equal vote in the upper house of the legislature. Each state would be represented in the lower house based on population.

THREE-FIFTHS COMPROMISE

The **Three-Fifths Compromise** satisfied northerners, who wanted the number of slaves in southern states to determine taxes but not representation. It also satisfied southern delegates, who wanted slaves counted as part of their state populations to increase their power. The delegates agreed to end the slave trade in 20 years.

> Underline the sentence that explains what action the delegates took about the slave trade.

A NEW SYSTEM OF GOVERNMENT

While most delegates wanted a strong central government, they also wanted to protect **popular sovereignty**. They thought **federalism** could accomplish that. States would control government functions not assigned to the federal government. The Constitution balances power among the **legislative branch**, the **executive branch**, and the **judicial branch**. The Constitution's framers established **checks and balances** to prevent any one branch from becoming too strong. The framers also provided a method for amending, or changing, the Constitution. These changes are called **amendments.**

> What do you think about checks and balances?
>
> _____
> _____
> _____

CHALLENGE ACTIVITY

Critical Thinking: Making Judgments Decide whether you support the Three-Fifths Compromise. Give a two-minute speech about your view.

DIRECTIONS Match the terms in the first column with their correct definitions from the second column by placing the letter of the correct definition in the space provided before each term.

_____ 1. checks and balances

_____ 2. Constitutional Convention

_____ 3. Great Compromise

_____ 4. James Madison

_____ 5. New Jersey Plan

_____ 6. popular sovereignty

_____ 7. Three-Fifths Compromise

_____ 8. Virginia Plan

_____ 9. federalism

_____ 10. legislative branch

a. meeting where delegates discussed ways to improve the Articles of Confederation

b. the sharing of power between a central government and the states it is comprised of

c. called the Father of the Constitution

d. called for a bicameral legislature with representation in both houses based on population

e. responsible for proposing and passing laws

f. called for a one-house legislature in which each state had an equal number of votes

g. gave each state an equal vote in the upper house of the legislature while granting to the lower house representation based on population

h. agreement that only part of the slave population of a state would be used when determining representation

i. the idea that political authority belongs to the people

j. system by which any one branch of government is prevented from becoming too powerful

Guided Reading Workbook

Forming a Government

Section 4

MAIN IDEAS
1. Federalists and Antifederalists engaged in debate over the new Constitution.
2. The *Federalist Papers* played an important role in the fight for ratification of the Constitution.
3. Ten amendments were added to the Constitution to provide a Bill of Rights to protect citizens.

Key Terms and People

Antifederalists people who opposed the Constitution

George Mason delegate who opposed the Constitution

Federalists people who supported the Constitution

Federalist Papers essays supporting the Constitution

amendments official changes to a document

Bill of Rights Constitutional amendments that protect the rights of citizens

Academic Vocabulary

advocate to plead in favor of

Section Summary

FEDERALISTS AND ANTIFEDERALISTS

Antifederalists believed that the Constitutional Convention should not have formed a new government. Delegate **George Mason** opposed the Constitution because it did not contain a section that guaranteed individual rights.

Most **Federalists** thought that the Constitution provided a good balance of power. Many wealthy planters, farmers, and lawyers were Federalists. Yet, many craftspeople, merchants, and poor workers also backed the Constitution. Several groups made speeches to **advocate** their views.

> Why did George Mason oppose the Constitution?
> _____
> _____
> _____

FEDERALIST PAPERS

The *Federalist Papers* were written anonymously by Alexander Hamilton, James Madison, and John

Jay in defense of the Constitution. They tried to persuade people that the Constitution would not overwhelm the states. Madison stated that the diversity of the United States meant no single group would take over the government.

The Constitution needed only nine states to pass it, but each state should ratify it as a way of proclaiming national unity. Every state except Rhode Island held state conventions that gave citizens the right to discuss and vote on the Constitution. On December 7, 1787, Delaware became the first state to ratify it. The Constitution went into effect in June 1788 after New Hampshire became the ninth state to ratify it. Several states ratified the Constitution only after a bill protecting individual rights was promised.

Why did states hold constitutional conventions?
_____
_____

What kind of bill did several states demand?
_____
_____

BILL OF RIGHTS

Many Antifederalists did not believe that the Constitution would safeguard personal rights. In the first session of Congress, James Madison spurred the legislators to develop a bill of rights. The rights would then become **amendments** to the Constitution after a two-thirds majority of both houses of Congress and three-fourths of the states approved them. Article V of the Constitution spelled out this way of changing the document to respond to the will of the people.

In December 1791 Congress proposed 12 amendments and turned them over to the states for ratification. By December 1791 the states had ratified the **Bill of Rights**. Ten of the proposed 12 amendments were written to protect citizens' rights. These amendments show how the Constitution was amended to meet the needs of a growing nation.

Why do you think the Constitution has lasted more than 200 years?
_____
_____

CHALLENGE ACTIVITY

Critical Thinking: Comparing and Contrasting
Write a short essay comparing and contrasting the views of Federalists and Antifederalists. Use specific examples.

DIRECTIONS Read each sentence and fill in the blank with the word
in the word pair that best completes the sentence.

1. A group of essays that defended the Constitution was the

   _____. (Bill of Rights/*Federalist Papers*)

2. _____ was an Antifederalist who felt the Constitution
   needed a bill of rights. (George Mason/Alexander Hamilton)

3. The _____, established a clear precedent for amending the
   Constitution. (Bill of Rights/*Federalist Papers*)

4. Supporters of the Constitution were known as _____.
   (Federalists/Antifederalists)

5. People who felt the Constitutional Convention should not have created a new

   government were called _____. (Federalists/Antifederalists)

6. _____ defended the Constitution in the *Federalist Papers*.
   (George Mason/Alexander Hamilton)

7. Official changes to the Constitution are called _____.
   (Bill of Rights/amendments)

Citizenship and the Constitution

Section 1

MAIN IDEAS

1. The framers of the Constitution devised the federal system.
2. The legislative branch makes the nation's laws.
3. The executive branch enforces the nation's laws.
4. The judicial branch determines whether or not laws are constitutional.

Key Terms and People

federal system the government system that gives certain powers to the federal government

impeach vote to bring charges of serious crimes against a president

veto cancel

executive orders commands from the president that have the power of law

pardons orders from the president that grant freedom from punishment

Thurgood Marshall the first African American Supreme Court Justice, appointed in 1967

Sandra Day O'Connor the first female Supreme Court Justice, appointed in 1981

Academic Vocabulary

distinct separate

Section Summary

THE FEDERAL SYSTEM

Under the **federal system**, the U.S. Constitution divides powers between the states and the federal government. The Constitution gives the federal government delegated powers, including coining money. It gives state governments or citizens reserved powers, including forming local governments. Concurrent powers are shared by federal and state governments. These powers include taxing.

Congress has added powers under the elastic clause to handle new issues.

> **Describe concurrent powers.**
> _____
> _____

LEGISLATIVE BRANCH

The federal government has three branches, each with **distinct** responsibilities. Congress, the legislative branch, has two parts. The House of Representatives has 435 members. A state's population determines the number of representatives for that state. Each state has two senators. They are elected statewide and represent the interests of the entire state.

> **What determines each state's number of representatives?**
> _____
> _____

EXECUTIVE BRANCH

This branch enforces laws made by Congress. The president heads the branch. Americans elect a president every four years. Presidents are limited to two terms. The House of Representatives can **impeach** the president. The Senate tries the cases. Congress dismisses the president if he or she is found guilty.

The president and Congress work together. A president can **veto** a law passed by Congress. Congress can undo a veto with a two-thirds majority vote. The president issues **executive orders** to carry out laws affecting the Constitution and other areas. The president also issues **pardons**.

> **How can Congress undo a presidential veto?**
> _____
> _____

JUDICIAL BRANCH

A system of federal courts with the U.S. Supreme Court at the head makes up this branch. Federal courts can undo a state or federal law if the court finds it unconstitutional. Congress can then change the law to make it constitutional.

If someone thinks a conviction was unfair, he or she can take the case to the court of appeals. The losing side in that trial may appeal the decision to the U.S. Supreme Court. If the Court declines to hear a case, the court of appeals decision is final. The Supreme Court has become more diverse with the appointments of **Thurgood Marshall** and **Sandra Day O'Connor**.

> **Why might a president appoint more diverse Justices?**
> _____
> _____

CHALLENGE ACTIVITY

Critical Thinking: Judging Would you prefer to serve in the House or the Senate during an impeachment? Write a brief essay explaining why.

DIRECTIONS On the line provided before each statement, write **T** if a statement is true and **F** if a statement is false. If the statement is false, rewrite it on the line provided so that it is a true statement.

_____ 1. The House of Representatives can impeach a president.

_____

_____ 2. Congress can veto a law that the President passes.

_____

_____ 3. The powers granted by the Constitution to the federal government are called delegated powers.

_____

_____ 4. A vote to bring charges of "treason, bribery, or other high crimes and misdemeanors" against a president is called impeachment.

_____

_____ 5. Sandra Day O'Connor became the first African American justice on the Supreme Court.

_____

_____ 6. The powers kept by the state governments or the citizens are called delegated powers.

_____

_____ 7. A president of the United States has been impeached.

_____

_____ 8. Thurgood Marshall became the first African American president of the United States.

_____

_____

Guided Reading Workbook

Citizenship and the Constitution

MAIN IDEAS
1. The First Amendment guarantees basic freedoms to individuals.
2. Other amendments focus on protecting citizens from certain abuses.
3. The rights of the accused are an important part of the Bill of Rights.
4. The rights of states and citizens are protected by the Bill of Rights.

Key Terms and People

James Madison a Federalist who promised that a Bill of Rights would be added to the Constitution

majority rule the idea that the greatest number of people in a society can make policies for everyone

petition a request made of the government

search warrant an order authorities must get before they search someone's property

due process a rule that the law must be fairly applied

indict formally accuse

double jeopardy a rule that says a person cannot be tried for the same crime more than once

eminent domain the government's power to take personal property to benefit the public

Section Summary
FIRST AMENDMENT

James Madison began writing a list of amendments to the Constitution in 1789. The states ratified 10 amendments, called the Bill of Rights. **Majority rule** could take away smaller groups' rights. The Bill of Rights protects all citizens. First Amendment rights include freedom of religion, freedom of the press, freedom of speech, freedom of assembly, and the right to **petition**. The U.S. government cannot support or interfere with the practice of a religion.

The freedoms of speech and the press give Americans the right to express their own ideas and hear those of others. Freedom of assembly means Americans may hold lawful meetings. Citizens can petition for new laws.

> **What does the Bill of Rights do?**
> _____
> _____

PROTECTING CITIZENS

The Second, Third, and Fourth Amendments stem from colonial problems with Britain. The Second Amendment gives state militias the right to bear arms in emergencies. The Third Amendment protects citizens against housing soldiers. The Fourth Amendment protects against certain "searches and seizures." Authorities must obtain a **search warrant** to enter a citizen's property.

> **When is a search warrant needed?**
> _____
> _____

RIGHTS OF THE ACCUSED

The Fifth, Sixth, Seventh, and Eighth Amendments guard the rights of the accused. The Fifth Amendment says that the government cannot take a person's life, liberty, or property without **due process**. A grand jury decides whether to **indict** a person. No one can face **double jeopardy**. Under **eminent domain** the government must pay owners a fair amount for their property.

The Sixth Amendment protects an indicted person's rights. The Seventh Amendment says that juries can decide civil cases, usually about money or property. The Eighth Amendment allows bail, or money defendants pay if they fail to appear in court. This amendment also prevents "cruel and unusual punishments" against a person convicted of a crime.

> **Predict a situation in which a government might exercise its right of eminent domain.**
> _____
> _____
> _____

RIGHTS OF STATES AND CITIZENS

The Ninth Amendment states that all citizens' rights are not given by the Constitution. According to the Tenth Amendment, any powers not delegated to the federal government or prohibited to the states are held by the states and the people.

> **What powers are held by the states and the people?**
> _____
> _____

CHALLENGE ACTIVITY

Critical Thinking: Developing In a small group, draw up a new law for which you would like to petition a government official.

DIRECTIONS Write two adjectives or descriptive phrases that describe the term.

1. double jeopardy _____

2. due process _____

3. eminent domain _____

4. indict _____

5. James Madison _____

6. petition _____

7. search warrant _____

DIRECTIONS Write a word or phrase that means the opposite of the term given.

8. indict _____

9. due process _____

10. majority rule _____

Citizenship and the Constitution

> **MAIN IDEAS**
> 1. Citizenship in the United States is determined in several ways.
> 2. Citizens are expected to fulfill a number of important duties.
> 3. Active citizen involvement in government and the community is encouraged.

Key Terms and People

naturalized citizens foreign-born people who: a) live in the United States, b) whose parents are not citizens, and c) who complete the requirements for U.S. citizenship

deport return to an immigrant's country of origin

draft required military service

political action committees groups that collect money for candidates who support certain issues

interest groups groups sharing interests that motivate them to take political action

Academic Vocabulary

influence to change or have an effect on

Section Summary

GAINING U.S. CITIZENSHIP

Naturalized citizens may become full citizens. They apply for and go through a process that can lead to citizenship. Then they have most of the rights and responsibilities of other citizens. Legal immigrants have many of those rights but cannot vote or hold public office. The U.S. government can **deport** immigrants who break the law. Legal immigrants over age 18 may seek naturalization after living in the U.S. for five years. After completing the requirements, the person takes an oath of allegiance to the United States and receives a certificate of naturalization. Unlike native-born citizens, and naturalized citizens can lose their citizenships and can't be president or vice president.

What limits exist on the rights of legal immigrants?
_____
_____

What happens after the oath of allegiance is taken?
_____
_____

RESPONSIBILITIES OF CITIZENSHIP

Citizens have duties as well as rights. They must obey laws and authority. They must pay taxes for services, including public roads and schools. Many pay a tax on their income to the federal government. Men 18 years or older must register with selective service in case of a **draft**. Citizens also have responsibilities to fulfill. Voting in elections is one of the most important responsibilities. Before voting, a citizen should learn about issues and candidates. Many media sources offer information; some may be deliberately biased. Staying informed on issues is a basic part of the national identity.

Why do citizens have duties along with rights?
_____
_____
_____

FIRST AMENDMENT RIGHTS

This amendment allows people to practice any religion they want or no religion at all. It allows citizens the freedom to express their views in speech and in the press. Two other important rights protected by this amendment are the right to assemble and to petition the government, rights that relate back to British policies toward the colonies.

Underline the sentence that describes the media

CITIZENS AND GOVERNMENT

Political participation is a national tradition. Some U.S. citizens work with **interest groups** that support a particular cause. Others help with donations to **political action committees** (PACs). Many Americans also volunteer in community service groups, such as local firefighters or law enforcement. A simple act such as picking up trash in a park can help a community.

Why is community service important and valuable?
_____
_____
_____

CHALLENGE ACTIVITY

Critical Thinking: Analyzing What connects a citizen's rights and responsibilities? Design a graphic organizer showing connections.

DIRECTIONS Write two adjectives or descriptive phrases that
describe the term.

1. interest groups _____

2. immigrants _____

3. political action committees _____

4. naturalized citizens _____

5. draft _____

deport	draft	political action committees
immigrants	interest groups	naturalized citizens

DIRECTIONS Use the six vocabulary words above to write a summary
of what you learned in the section.

_____

_____

_____

_____

_____

_____

_____

_____

Launching the Nation

MAIN IDEAS
1. In 1789 George Washington became the first president of the United States.
2. Congress and the president organized the executive and judicial branches of government.
3. Americans had high expectations of their new government.

Key Terms and People

George Washington an honest leader, a hero of the revolution, and the first U.S. president

electoral college a group of delegates, or electors, who represent the people's vote in choosing the president

Martha Washington George Washington's wife and the First Lady

precedent an action or a decision that later serves as an example

Judiciary Act of 1789 an act that created three levels of federal courts and defined their powers and relationships to the state courts ·

Academic Vocabulary

agreement a decision reached by two or more people or groups

Section Summary

THE FIRST PRESIDENT

George Washington was unanimously elected by the **electoral college** in January 1789. John Adams became his vice president. **Martha Washington** entertained and accompanied her husband at social events. She was in charge of the presidential household. Other women, such as Abigail Adams, wife of John Adams, believed women needed to play a larger role in the nation than Martha Washington did. They thought that women should take a more important role in society because they educated their children to be good citizens.

> Why did some women support a larger national role for women?
>
> _____
> _____
> _____

ORGANIZING THE GOVERNMENT

The new federal government had to establish a **precedent** when creating policies and procedures that would have a great influence on the future of the nation. Congress formed departments in the executive branch to oversee various areas of national policy. Washington consulted with department heads, or cabinet members, who advised him. Our presidents today also meet with their key advisers.

> **What did cabinet members provide for the president?**
> _____
> _____

Congress passed the **Judiciary Act of 1789**. This act created the federal court system and the courts' location. The president nominates candidates for federal judgeships. The Senate holds the power to approve or reject the candidates.

> **What limited the president's ability to nominate federal judges?**
> _____
> _____
> _____

AMERICANS' EXPECTATIONS OF GOVERNMENT

Americans had high expectations of their government. They wanted trade that did not have the limits put in place by the British Parliament. They also expected the government to protect them and keep the economy strong.

In 1790 four million people lived in the United States. Most Americans worked on farms. They hoped for fair taxes and the right to move onto western lands. Americans who lived in towns worked as craftspeople, laborers, or merchants. They wanted help with their businesses. Merchants wanted simpler trade laws. Manufacturers wanted laws to shield them from overseas competitors.

> **Underline the sentences that explain the contrast between what country residents and town residents wanted.**

Most cities were small. Only New York and Philadelphia topped 25,000 residents. New York City, the first capital, reflected the new nation's spirit. In 1792 some 24 Wall Street stockbrokers signed an **agreement** that eventually created the New York Stock Exchange.

> **In what year was the agreement signed that led to the New York Stock Exchange?**

CHALLENGE ACTIVITY

Critical Thinking: Evaluating You have just attended George Washington's inauguration. Write a letter to a friend describing your thoughts about him.

| electoral college | Judiciary Act of 1789 | precedent |
| George Washington | Martha Washington | |

DIRECTIONS Answer each question by writing a sentence that contains at least one word from the word bank.

1. What did Congress pass to set up the number of federal courts and their locations?

_____

_____

_____

_____

2. Who had to entertain guests and attend social events with the president of the United States?

_____

_____

_____

_____

3. What was the group of delegates called that was sent to choose the first president of the United States?

_____

_____

_____

_____

4. What do we call an action or a decision that later serves as an example?

_____

_____

_____

_____

Launching the Nation

Section 2

MAIN IDEAS

1. Hamilton tackled the problem of settling national and state debt.
2. Thomas Jefferson opposed Hamilton's views on government and the economy.
3. Hamilton created a national bank to strengthen the U.S. economy.

Key Terms and People

Alexander Hamilton the first secretary of the U.S. treasury who wanted to pay the nation's foreign debt immediately and gradually repay the full value of all bonds

national debt money owed by the United States

bonds certificates that represent money

speculators people who buy items at low prices in the hope that the value will rise

Thomas Jefferson the first secretary of state who thought that repaying the full value of all bonds would cheat bondholders who had sold their bonds at low prices

loose construction the view that the federal government can take reasonable actions that the Constitution does not specifically forbid

strict construction the view that the federal government should do only what the Constitution specifically says it can do

The Bank of the United States the national bank

Section Summary
SETTLING THE DEBT

Alexander Hamilton wanted to pay off the **national debt**. He figured that the United States owed $11.7 million to foreign countries. The nation also owed about $40.4 million to U.S. citizens.

During the Revolutionary War the government sold **bonds** to raise money. Officials said bonds would be repurchased at a higher price. Some bondholders sold their bonds to **speculators**. Hamilton and **Thomas Jefferson** disagreed on what to do. More politicians agreed with Hamilton. The government replaced old bonds with new, more reliable ones.

> How did the government raise money during the Revolution?
>
> _____
>
> _____

Hamilton thought that the federal government should repay $21.5 million of the states' debt. But southern leaders objected. Their states had relatively low debts. Hamilton arranged to have the U.S. capital's location changed from New York to Philadelphia and finally Washington, D.C. Southern leaders then supported his plan.

> **How did Hamilton persuade the southern leaders?**
> _____
> _____

JEFFERSON OPPOSES HAMILTON

Hamilton and Jefferson disagreed about the role of the central government. Hamilton wanted a strong federal government. Jefferson wanted strong powers for the states. Hamilton did not want people to have much power because he had little faith in the average person. Jefferson believed that the people had the right to rule the country. Hamilton backed manufacturing, business, and higher tariffs. Jefferson backed farming and lower tariffs.

> **Underline the sentences that explain Hamilton's and Jefferson's views of the American people.**

A NATIONAL BANK

In 1791 Hamilton and Jefferson disagreed about the government's economic problems. Hamilton wanted a national bank so the government could safely deposit money. Jefferson believed that Hamilton's plan gave too much power to the federal government. Hamilton supported **loose construction** of the Constitution. Jefferson backed **strict construction**. Washington and Congress wanted **The Bank of the United States**. It helped make the U.S. economy more stable.

> **Name one reason Hamilton supported a national bank.**
> _____
> _____

> **Do you think the Bank was a good idea? Why or why not?**
> _____
> _____

CHALLENGE ACTIVITY

Critical Thinking: Evaluation Do you think Hamilton or Jefferson was more correct in his views of people? Give a brief speech explaining your opinion.

DIRECTIONS Read each sentence and fill in the blank with the word
in the word pair that best completes the sentence.

1. _____ disagreed with the idea to pay speculators the full
   value of the government bonds that they had bought during the Revolutionary
   War. (Thomas Jefferson/Alexander Hamilton)

2. Hamilton's view of the Constitution was called _____.
   (loose construction /strict construction)

3. Congress chartered the _____ which played an important
   role in making the U.S. economy more stable.
   (national debt/Bank of the United States)

4. _____ are people who buy items at low prices in the hope
   that the value will rise. (Bonds/Speculators)

5. A _____ of the Constitution allows the federal government
   to take reasonable actions that the Constitution does not specifically forbid.
   (loose construction /strict construction)

6. People who favor _____ of the Constitution believe the
   federal government should do only what the Constitution says it can do.
   (loose construction /strict construction)

7. The amount of money that was owed by the United States was called the

   _____. (national debt/Bank of the United States)

8. The secretary of the treasury who had to deal with the challenge of paying off the

   national debt was _____.

   (Thomas Jefferson/Alexander Hamilton)

9. _____ are certificates that represent money.
   (Bonds/Speculators)

10. Thomas Jefferson's view of the Constitution was known as

    _____. (loose construction /strict construction)

Launching the Nation

Section 3

MAIN IDEAS
1. The United States tried to remain neutral regarding events in Europe.
2. The United States and Native Americans came into conflict in the Northwest Territory.
3. The Whiskey Rebellion tested Washington's administration.
4. In his Farewell Address, President Washington advised the nation.

Key Terms and People

French Revolution a rebellion of the French people against their king that led to the creation of a republican government

Neutrality Proclamation a formal statement that the United States would not take sides with any European countries who were at war

privateers private ships hired by a country to attack its enemies

Jay's Treaty an agreement that settled the disputes between United States and Britain in the early 1790s

Pinckney's Treaty an agreement that settled border and trade disputes with Spain

Little Turtle a Native American chief who fought against U.S. forces in 1790

Battle of Fallen Timbers the battle that broke the strength of Native American forces in the Northwest Territory

Treaty of Greenville an agreement that gave the United States right of entry to American Indian lands

Whiskey Rebellion uprising in which some farmers refused to pay the whiskey tax

Academic Vocabulary

neutral unbiased, not favoring either side in a conflict

Section Summary
REMAINING NEUTRAL

The **French Revolution** increased tensions between France and Britain. Many Americans supported the French Revolution, but others opposed it. France and Great Britain finally went to war. George Washington believed the United States should be **neutral** and issued the **Neutrality Proclamation**. A French representative asked American sailors to command **privateers** to aid France in fighting England.

Why might some Americans support the French Revolution?
_____
_____

Washington said that this violated U.S. neutrality. Jefferson thought the United States should support France and resented interference in his role as secretary of state. He resigned in 1793.

Washington wanted to stop a war between the United States and Britain. The two sides signed **Jay's Treaty**. Britain would pay damages on seized American ships. **Pinckney's Treaty**, signed with Spain, settled the issue of Florida's border and reopened New Orleans to American ships.

> **What did the United States gain from Pinckney's Treaty?**
> _____

CONFLICT IN THE NORTHWEST TERRITORY

Americans continued to settle the territory despite protests of American Indians. U.S. forces lost a battle to Miami chief **Little Turtle**. But General Anthony Wayne commanded U.S. troops in gaining the territory at last. The American Indians were defeated in the **Battle of Fallen Timber** and their leaders signed the **Treaty of Greenville** a year later.

> **Why might Americans Indians have protested the U.S. settlements?**
> _____
> _____

THE WHISKEY REBELLION

In March 1791 Congress passed a tax on American-made whiskey. The **Whiskey Rebellion** broke out. Washington personally led the army against the rebels in western Pennsylvania, but they fled. The revolt ended with no battle.

WASHINGTON SAYS FAREWELL

Washington declined to run for a third term. He had tired of public life and considered the American people the nation's leaders. In his farewell speech, he warned about the dangers of foreign ties and political conflicts at home. He also cautioned against too much debt. At the conclusion of his speech, he stated that he looked forward to a life "of good laws under a free government. . ."

> **Name two dangers that Washington mentioned.**
> _____
> _____

CHALLENGE ACTIVITY

Critical Thinking: Sequencing Create a timeline of important events in the 1790s. Describe each of the events and explain how one event caused or resulted from another event. Illustrate your timeline.

Guided Reading Workbook

DIRECTIONS Match the terms in the first column with their correct definitions from the second column by placing the letter of the correct definition in the space provided before each term.

_____ 1. Battle of Fallen Timbers

_____ 2. Edmund Genet

_____ 3. French Revolution

_____ 4. Jay's Treaty

_____ 5. Little Turtle

_____ 6. Neutrality Proclamation

_____ 7. Pinckney's Treaty

_____ 8. privateers

_____ 9. Treaty of Greenville

_____ 10. Whiskey Rebellion

a. private ships used to attack a nation's enemies

b. The storming of the Bastille was one of the first acts of this event that also overthrew the king.

c. where protesters refused to pay a tax and even tarred and feathered tax collectors

d. where American Indians fought the U.S. Army; named for an area where many trees had once been destroyed by a tornado

e. ended the frontier war and gave the United States right of entry to American Indian lands in the Northwest Territory

f. France's new representative to the United States that asked American seamen to command privateers

g. said that Spain agreed to change the Florida border and that Spain's government would reopen the port at New Orleans to American ships

h. stated that the United States would not take sides with any European countries who were at war with one another

i. led an American Indian group that defeated U.S. forces in the Northwest Territory

j. signed by the United States and Great Britain; stated that the British would pay damages on seized American ships; the United States agreed to pay pre-Revolutionary debts it owed the British

Launching the Nation

> **MAIN IDEAS**
> 1. The rise of political parties created competition in the election of 1796.
> 2. The XYZ affair caused problems for President John Adams.
> 3. Controversy broke out over the Alien and Sedition Acts.

Key Terms and People

political parties groups that help elect people and shape politics

Federalist Party a political group that wanted a strong federal government and supported industry and trade

Democratic-Republican Party a political group that wanted to limit the federal government's powers

XYZ affair a French demand for a $250,000 bribe and a $12 million loan in exchange for a treaty

Alien and Sedition Acts laws that punished supporters of France and deprived people of the freedom to say and write what they believed.

Kentucky and Virginia Resolutions formal statements that the Alien and Sedition Acts were unconstitutional

Section Summary

THE ELECTION OF 1796

In the election of 1796, more than one candidate ran for president. **Political parties** had started during Washington's presidency. Washington cautioned against party rivalry in his farewell, but rivalry dominated the 1796 election.

Alexander Hamilton was key in founding the **Federalist Party**. John Adams and Thomas Pinckney were the Federalist candidates. Thomas Jefferson and James Madison helped found the **Democratic-Republican Party**. That party selected Thomas Jefferson and Aaron Burr as its candidates.

Business people in cities tended to support Adams. Farmers generally favored Jefferson. Both sides attacked each other. Adams won; Jefferson was second. He and Jefferson then had to serve as president and vice president.

> Who helped start the Federalist Party?
>
> _____
>
> _____

PRESIDENT ADAMS AND THE XYZ AFFAIR

Adams made improving the relationship between the United States and France a high priority. France was unhappy when the United States refused to let its citizens join in the war against Britain. Adams sent U.S. diplomats to repair that problem and make a treaty to guard U.S. shipping. The French foreign minister refused to meet with them.

Three French agents said that the minister would discuss a treaty only if America paid a $250,000 bribe and gave a $12 million loan. The American public became furious about the **XYZ affair**. Still, Adams did not declare war on France. This angered many other Federalists. At last the United States and France did negotiate a peace treaty.

> Based on what you have read, what do you think Adams's view of France was?
>
> _____
>
> _____

> In the end, what occurred between the United States and France?
>
> _____
>
> _____

THE ALIEN AND SEDITION ACTS

The **Alien and Sedition Acts**, passed by Federalists in Congress, became law in 1798. The Alien Act empowered the president to remove foreign residents he decided were involved in any treasonable or secret plots against the government. The Sedition Act forbid U.S. residents to "write, print, utter, or publish" false or critical words against the government.

The **Kentucky and Virginia Resolutions** stated that the acts were unconstitutional. Jefferson and James Madison said that the states could disobey unconstitutional federal laws. Congress did not repeal the acts, though they were not renewed. The resolutions presented the view that states could dispute the federal government. Later politicians would say this idea meant that the states could declare laws or actions of the federal government to be illegal.

> Underline the sentence that explains what the Sedition Act did.

CHALLENGE ACTIVITY

Critical Thinking: Predicting Do some research to discover when in U.S. history states would say that they could declare federal law to be illegal. Write a brief essay explaining both sides of the argument.

DIRECTIONS Read each sentence and fill in the blank with the word in the word pair that best completes the sentence.

1. The president was allowed to remove foreign residents he thought were involved

   "in any treasonable or secret machinations against the government" by the

   _____. (Alien Act/Sedition Act)

2. The _____ said United States citizens could not "write, print,
   utter or publish" false or hostile words against the government.
   (Alien Act/Sedition Act)

3. The bribe offer where French agents made unreasonable demands to U.S.

   diplomats is called the _____. (Federalist Party/XYZ Affair)

4. Thomas Jefferson and James Madison helped start the _____
   whose members were called Republicans.
   (Federalist Party/Democratic-Republican Party)

5. Alexander Hamilton helped found the _____ which wanted
   a strong federal government. (Federalist Party/Democratic-Republican Party)

DIRECTIONS On the line provided before each statement, write **T** if a
statement is true and **F** if a statement is false. If the statement is false,
write the correct term on the line after each sentence that makes the
sentence a true statement.

_____ 6. Groups that help elect people and shape policies are called the Alien and
          Sedition Acts.

          _____

_____ 7. The Federalist Party helped Alexander Hamilton, the man who helped
          found the party, get elected president of the United States.

          _____

_____ 8. The Republicans chose in 1796 Thomas Jefferson and Aaron Burr as their
          candidates.

          _____

MAIN IDEAS

1. The election of 1800 marked the first peaceful transition in power from one political party to another.

2. President Jefferson's beliefs about the federal government were reflected in his policies.

3. *Marbury* v. *Madison* increased the power of the judicial branch of government.

Key Terms and People

John Adams Federalist president first elected in 1796 who lost the 1800 presidential election

Thomas Jefferson Republican who defeated John Adams in the presidential election of 1800

John Marshall a Federalist appointed by Adams to be Chief Justice of the Supreme Court

Marbury **v.** *Madison* a case that established the Supreme Court's power of judicial review

judicial review the Supreme Court's power to declare an act of Congress unconstitutional

Academic Vocabulary

functions uses or purposes

Section Summary

THE ELECTION OF 1800

Thomas Jefferson defeated **John Adams** and became president in 1800. In campaigning, both sides had made their cases in newspaper editorials and letters. Both sides believed that if the other gained power, the nation would be destroyed.

The campaigning was intense. Federalists said if Jefferson gained power, revolution and chaos would follow. Republicans claimed that Adams would crown himself king. Jefferson and Aaron Burr, his vice presidential running mate, each won 73 votes. After the thirty-sixth ballot in the House of Representatives, Jefferson was elected President.

How did the presidential candidates wage the campaign of 1800?
_____
_____

JEFFERSON'S POLICIES

Jefferson gave his first speech in the new capitol. He said he supported the will of the majority. He emphasized his belief in a limited government and the protection of civil liberties. Jefferson convinced Congress to let the Alien and Sedition Acts expire. He cut military spending to free money to pay the national debt. The Republican-led Congress passed laws to end the unpopular whiskey tax and other domestic taxes.

In 1801 the national government was made up of only several hundred people. Jefferson liked it that way. He thought that safeguarding the nation against foreign threats, delivering the mail, and collecting custom duties were the most important **functions** of the federal government. Jefferson had fought Alexander Hamilton over the creation of the Bank of the United States, but he did not close it.

> **Name one action Jefferson took based on his principles.**
> _____
> _____

MARBURY V. MADISON

Adams filled 16 new federal judgeships with Federalists before leaving office. Republicans in Congress soon repealed the Judiciary Act upon which Adams's appointments were based. A controversy arose when Adams appointed William Marbury as a justice of the peace. The documents supporting Marbury's appointment were never delivered.

When Jefferson took office, secretary of state James Madison would not deliver them. Marbury sued and asked the Supreme Court to order Madison to give him the documents. **John Marshall** wrote the Court's opinion in *Marbury* **v.** *Madison*. He ruled that the law which Marbury's case depended upon was unconstitutional. The case established the Court's power of **judicial review**.

> **Why did Marbury sue Madison?**
> _____
> _____

CHALLENGE ACTIVITY

Critical Thinking: Making Inferences What if the 1800 campaign were waged as campaigns are waged now? Write a speech that you think Thomas Jefferson would give. Deliver his speech.

| John Adams | judicial review | Thomas Jefferson |
| John Marshall | *Marbury* v. *Madison* | |

DIRECTIONS Answer each question by writing a sentence that contains at least one word from the word bank.

1. Who was the Chief Justice of the Supreme Court that disagreed with President Jefferson about many political issues?

_____

_____

_____

2. Who ran against Thomas Jefferson in the election of 1800?

_____

_____

_____

3. The power of judicial review was established by the U.S. Supreme Court's decision in what case?

_____

_____

_____

4. What was the outcome of the presidential election of 1800?

_____

_____

_____

MAIN IDEAS

1. As American settlers moved West, control of the Mississippi River became more important to the United States.

2. The Louisiana Purchase almost doubled the size of the United States.

3. Expeditions led by Lewis, Clark, and Pike increased Americans' understanding of the West.

Key Terms and People

Louisiana Purchase the purchase of Louisiana from France for $15 million, which roughly doubled the size of the United States

Meriwether Lewis a former army captain chosen by Jefferson to lead an expedition to explore the West

William Clark co-leader of the western expedition

Lewis and Clark expedition a long journey to explore the Louisiana Purchase

Sacagawea a Shoshone who helped the expedition by naming plants and gathering edible fruits and vegetables for the group

Zebulon Pike an explorer of the West who reached the summit of the mountain now known as Pike's Peak

Section Summary

AMERICAN SETTLERS MOVE WEST

Thousands of Americans moved into the area between the Appalachians and the Mississippi River. The setters used the Mississippi and Ohio rivers to move their products to eastern markets. Jefferson was concerned that a foreign power might shut down the port of New Orleans, which settlers needed to move their goods East and to Europe. Spain governed New Orleans and Louisiana, which extended from the Mississippi to the Rocky Mountains. Under a secret treaty, Spain gave Louisiana to France, transferring the problem of trying to keep Americans out of Louisiana.

> **Why would Americans want to move into Louisiana?**
> _____
> _____

> **Why did Jefferson worry about the port of New Orleans?**
> _____
> _____

LOUISIANA

In 1802, before giving Louisiana to France, Spain shut American shipping out of New Orleans.

Jefferson sent U.S. representatives to France to buy New Orleans. Napoleon ruled France. He wanted to rebuild France's empire in North America. But Napoleon had no military base from which to enter Louisiana. He also needed money to wage war against Great Britain. The United States bought the western territory for $15 million in the **Louisiana Purchase**.

> **What are two reasons that Napoleon did not try to conquer Louisiana?**
>
> _____
>
> _____

EXPLORERS HEAD WEST

Western Native Americans and the land they lived on were a mystery. President Jefferson wanted to know about them and their land. He also wondered if there was a river route to the Pacific Ocean.

In 1803 Congress provided money to explore the West. **Meriwether Lewis** and **William Clark** were chosen to lead the **Lewis and Clark expedition**, which began in May 1804.

Lewis and Clark and their crew traveled up the Missouri River. Finally, they saw Native Americans, and Lewis used interpreters to tell their leaders that the United States now owned the land on which they lived. **Sacagawea** and her husband aided Lewis and Clark. Lewis and Clark did not find a river route to the Pacific, but they learned much about western lands.

> **Underline the sentences that explain why Jefferson wanted to know more about the West.**

In 1806 **Zebulon Pike** was sent to locate the Red River, which was the Louisiana Territory's border with New Spain. In present-day Colorado he reached the summit of Pike's Peak. Spanish cavalry arrested him in Spanish-held lands and imprisoned him. When released he returned to the United States and reported on his trip. He gave many Americans their first information about the Southwest.

> **What was one obstacle faced by Pike on his expedition to the West?**
>
> _____
>
> _____

CHALLENGE ACTIVITY

Critical Thinking: Drawing Inferences Some members of the Lewis and Clark expedition kept journals or diaries. Write a brief diary entry as if you were a member of the expedition.

| Louisiana Purchase | Meriwether Lewis | Sacagawea |
| William Clark | Zebulon Pike | Lewis and Clark expedition |

DIRECTIONS Write two adjectives or descriptive phrases that describe the term.

1. Louisiana Purchase _____

2. Sacagawea _____

3. Lewis and Clark expedition _____

4. Zebulon Pike _____

5. William Clark _____

DIRECTIONS Choose five of the vocabulary words from the word list. Use these words to write a summary of what you learned in the section.

_____

_____

_____

_____

_____

_____

_____

The Jefferson Era

MAIN IDEAS
1. Violations of U.S. neutrality led Congress to enact a ban on trade.
2. Native Americans, Great Britain, and the United States came into conflict in the West.
3. The War Hawks led a growing call for war with Great Britain.

Key Terms and People

USS *Constitution* a large U.S. warship sent to end attacks by Mediterranean pirates on American merchant ships

impressment the practice of forcing people to serve in the army or navy

embargo the banning of trade

Embargo Act a U.S. law that essentially banned trade with all foreign countries

Non-Intercourse Act a new law banning only trade with Great Britain, France, and their colonies

Tecumseh a brilliant speaker who warned other Native Americans that settlers wanted their lands

Battle of Tippecanoe the battle between the U.S. forces and Tecumseh's followers that ended with the U.S. forces winning

War Hawks several members of Congress who called for war against Great Britain

James Madison a Republican who was elected president in 1808

Section Summary
VIOLATIONS OF NEUTRALITY

In the late 1700s and early 1800s, American merchant ships sailed the oceans. The profitable overseas trade was dangerous. Pirates seized cargo and held crews for ransom. The United States sent the **USS *Constitution*** and other ships to end the attacks.

When Great Britain and France declared war in 1803, each tried to stop the United States from selling goods to the other. The British and French searched many American ships for war goods. Then Britain started searching American ships for sailors who had deserted the British navy. At times U.S. citizens were seized by accident.

> **Why did Britain and France try to stop the United States from selling goods to the other?**
>
> _____
>
> _____

Impressment continued over U.S. protests. Thomas Jefferson, who had been re-elected in 1804, favored an **embargo** rather than war with Britain. Many feared that fighting Britain's vast navy would threaten U.S. independence. In late 1807 Congress passed the **Embargo Act** to punish Britain and France. American merchants lost huge amounts of money because of the act, which prevented merchants from selling goods to either nation. In 1809 Congress replaced the embargo with the **Non-Intercourse Act**. That law did not work either.

> **How was an embargo an alternative to war?**
> _____
> _____

CONFLICT IN THE WEST

In the West, Native Americans, the United States, and Great Britain clashed. As settlers poured into the West, Native Americans lost land that they believed was taken unfairly. British agents from Canada armed Native Americans in the West. **Tecumseh**, a Shawnee chief, united his forces with the Creek nation. William Henry Harrison, the governor of the Indiana Territory, raised an army to battle Tecumseh. At the day-long **Battle of Tippecanoe**, Harrison's forces defeated the army.

> **How did British agents aid Native Americans in the West?**
> _____
> _____

CALL FOR WAR

War Hawks in Congress led in demanding war against Britain. The leaders wanted to end British influence on Native Americans. They resented British restraints on U.S. trade. Others opposed war against Britain. They believed America lacked the military strength to win.

In 1808 Republican **James Madison** was elected president. He had difficulty carrying on the unpopular trade policy. In 1812 he asked Congress to vote on whether to wage war against Britain. Congress voted to declare war. Madison was re-elected and led the nation during the War of 1812.

> **Describe the problem that Madison faced in 1808.**
> _____
> _____
> _____

CHALLENGE ACTIVITY

Critical Thinking: Predicting List difficulties that the United States might face in the War of 1812.

DIRECTIONS Match the terms in the first column with their correct definitions from the second column by placing the letter of the correct definition in the space provided before each term.

_____ 1. Battle of Tippecanoe

_____ 2. embargo

_____ 3. Embargo Act

_____ 4. impressment

_____ 5. the *Chesapeake*

_____ 6. Non-Intercourse Act

_____ 7. Tecumseh

_____ 8. USS *Constitution*

_____ 9. War Hawks

_____ 10. James Madison

a. sent by the United States to bring an end to the attacks by the Barbary pirates

b. the act of forcing people to serve in the army or navy

c. the banning of trade with a country

d. act that banned trade by the United States with all foreign countries

e. act that banned trade with Britain, France, and their colonies

f. a Shawnee chief

g. the all-day battle that resulted in Tecumseh fleeing to Canada

h. group of congressmen, led by Henry Clay, who called for war against Britain

i. commander in chief of the United States during the War of 1812

j. U.S. Navy ship stopped by the British in 1807

The Jefferson Era

Section 4

MAIN IDEAS

1. American forces held their own against the British in the early battles of the war.
2. U.S. forces stopped British offensives in the East and South.
3. The effects of the war included prosperity and national pride.

Key Terms and People

Oliver Hazard Perry U.S. Navy commodore who won a victory against the British

Battle of Lake Erie the victory won by Perry and his sailors

Andrew Jackson the commander of the Tennessee militia who led an attack on the Creek nation in Alabama

Treaty of Fort Jackson the treaty that forced the Creek nation to give up millions of acres of their land

Battle of New Orleans the last major conflict of the War of 1812, which made Andrew Jackson a hero

Hartford Convention a meeting of Federalists opposed to the war

Treaty of Ghent the pact that ended the War of 1812

Academic Vocabulary

consequences the effects of a particular event or events

Section Summary

EARLY BATTLES

In 1812 the United States launched a war against a dominant nation. The British navy had hundreds of ships. The U.S. Navy had fewer than twenty ships, but it boasted expert sailors and big new warships. American morale rose when its ships defeated the British in several battles. Finally, the British blockaded U.S. seaports.

The U.S. planned to attack Canada from Detroit, from Niagara Falls, and from the Hudson River Valley toward Montreal. British soldiers and Native Americans led by Tecumseh took Fort Detroit. State militia doomed the other two attacks against Canada by arguing that they were not required to fight in a foreign country.

> Underline the sentences that contrast the U.S. and British navies.

Guided Reading Workbook

In 1813 the United States planned to end Britain's rule of Lake Erie. Commodore **Oliver Hazard Perry** and his small fleet won the **Battle of Lake Erie**. General Harrison then marched his troops into Canada. He defeated a combined force of British and Native Americans, breaking Britain's power. Tecumseh died in the fighting, harming the alliance of the British and the Native Americans.

In 1814 **Andrew Jackson** won a battle against the Creek nation that ended in the **Treaty of Fort Jackson**.

> **What effect did the death of Tecumseh have?**
> _____
> _____

GREAT BRITAIN ON THE OFFENSIVE

The British sent more troops to America after defeating the French in 1814. The British set fire to the White House and other buildings in Washington, D.C. The British also attacked New Orleans.

Andrew Jackson commanded forces made up of regular soldiers. They included two battalions of free African Americans, a group of Choctaw Indian militia, and pirates led by Jean Lafitte. Although Jackson's forces were outnumbered, America won the **Battle of New Orleans**, the last key battle of the war. Andrew Jackson became a war hero.

> **Why was Andrew Jackson considered a hero?**
> _____
> _____

EFFECTS OF THE WAR

Before Federalist delegates from the **Hartford Convention** reached Washington, the war had ended. Slow communications meant that neither Jackson nor the Federalists heard that the **Treaty of Ghent** finished the war. Each nation gave back the territory it had conquered. Yet the war had **consequences:** intense patriotism in America as well as growth of American manufacturing.

> **In what ways did the war benefit the United States?**
> _____
> _____
> _____

CHALLENGE ACTIVITY

Critical Thinking: Drawing Inferences You are the first mate on a New England trading ship several months after the War of 1812. Write a letter about how the end of the war affects you.

Andrew Jackson	Battle of New Orleans	Treaty of Ghent
Treaty of Fort Jackson	Hartford Convention	
Battle of Lake Erie	Oliver Hazard Perry	

DIRECTIONS Read each sentence and choose the correct term from the word bank to replace the underlined term. Write the underlined term in the space provided and then define the term in your own words.

1. The gathering of New England Federalists at Hartford, Connecticut to oppose

   war is referred to as the <u>Treaty of Ghent</u>. _____

   Your definition _____

   _____

   _____

2. The <u>Battle of New Orleans</u> forced the Creek Indians to give up millions of acres

   of their land. _____

   Your definition _____

   _____

   _____

3. <u>Oliver Hazard Perry</u> was the commander of the Tennessee militia, which

   included about 2,000 volunteers that attacked the Creek Indians. _____

   Your definition _____

   _____

   _____

4. <u>Andrew Jackson's</u> naval victory in the Battle of Lake Erie forced the British to

   withdraw and gave the U.S. Army new hope. _____

   Your definition _____

   _____

   _____

A New National Identity

MAIN IDEAS
1. The United States and Great Britain settled their disputes over boundaries and control of waterways.
2. The United States gained Florida in an agreement with Spain.
3. With the Monroe Doctrine, the United States strengthened its relationship with Latin America.

Key Terms and People

Rush-Bagot Agreement a compromise that limited U.S. and British naval power on the Great Lakes

Convention of 1818 a treaty that gave the United States fishing rights off parts of the Newfoundland and Labrador coasts

James Monroe U.S. president elected in 1816

Adams-Onís Treaty an agreement that settled all border disputes between the United States and Spain

Simon Bolívar the leader of the successful revolutions of Latin American colonies against Spain

Monroe Doctrine a statement of American policy warning European nations not to interfere with the Americas

Academic Vocabulary

circumstances surrounding situation

Section Summary

SETTLING DISPUTES WITH GREAT BRITAIN

After the War of 1812 ended, both the United States and Great Britain wanted to retain their navies and freedom to fish on the Great Lakes. The **Rush-Bagot Agreement** resolved that issue. The **Convention of 1818** gave America certain fishing rights, and it established the border between the United States and Canada. In this treaty, both countries agreed to occupy the Pacific Northwest together.

> **What were the results of the Convention of 1818?**
>
> _____
> _____

THE UNITED STATES GAINS FLORIDA

The United States also debated its border with Spanish Florida. President **James Monroe** sent General Andrew Jackson and troops to protect the U.S.-Florida border. Seminole Indians often aided runaway slaves and sometimes raided U.S. settlements. Under Jackson's command U.S. troops invaded Florida to catch Seminole raiders, starting the First Seminole War.

Jackson also captured most of Spain's key military posts. Jackson took these actions without a direct command from the president. The Spanish were upset, but most Americans backed Jackson. In 1819 Secretary of State John Quincy Adams and Spanish diplomat Luis de Onís negotiated the **Adams-Onís Treaty**. This treaty settled all border disputes between the United States and Spain.

> **Why did President Monroe send Jackson to Florida?**
> _____
> _____

> **What convinced the Spanish to negotiate with the Americans?**
> _____
> _____

MONROE DOCTRINE

By the early 1820s most Latin American countries had won independence from Spain. **Simon Bolívar**, called the Liberator, led many of these battles. The United States saw the **circumstances** as comparable to the American Revolution. United States leaders supported the Latin Americans in their struggles with European powers.

Monroe developed the **Monroe Doctrine** to guard against European countries interfering with the new Latin American nations. The document spells out the relationship between European nations and the United States in the Western Hemisphere. The doctrine states that the United States will intervene in Latin American affairs when American security is at risk. Few European nations challenged the doctrine.

> **Why did the United States support Latin American independence?**
> _____
> _____

CHALLENGE ACTIVITY

Critical Thinking: Cause and Effect Make a chart identifying the causes and effects of the Rush-Bagot Agreement, the Adams-Onís Treaty, and the Monroe Doctrine.

Adams-Onís Treaty	Convention of 1818	James Monroe
Monroe Doctrine	Rush-Bagot Agreement	Simon Bolívar

DIRECTIONS Write two adjectives or descriptive phrases that describe the term.

1. Monroe Doctrine _____

2. Convention of 1818 _____

3. James Monroe _____

4. Rush-Bagot Agreement _____

5. Simon Bolívar _____

DIRECTIONS Use the six vocabulary words to write a summary of what you learned in the section.

_____

_____

_____

_____

_____

_____

A New National Identity

Section 2

MAIN IDEAS
1. Growing nationalism led to improvements in the nation's transportation systems.
2. The Missouri Compromise settled an important regional conflict.
3. The outcome of the election of 1824 led to controversy.

Key Terms and People

nationalism a sense of pride and devotion to a nation

Henry Clay a U.S. representative from Kentucky who supported an emphasis on national unity

American System a series of measures intended to make the United States economically self-sufficient

Cumberland Road the first road built by the federal government

Erie Canal a waterway that ran from Albany to Buffalo, New York

Era of Good Feelings a U.S. era of peace, pride, and progress

sectionalism disagreement between leaders of different regions

Missouri Compromise an agreement that settled the conflict over Missouri's application for statehood

John Quincy Adams chosen as president by the House of Representatives in 1824

Academic Vocabulary

incentive something that leads people to action

Section Summary
GROWING NATIONALISM

Americans appreciated a rising sense of **nationalism** based on favorable negotiations with foreign nations. **Henry Clay** firmly supported this nationalism. Clay developed the **American System** to help create a stronger national economy and reduce regional disagreements. He pushed for a protective tariff and a national bank that would back a single currency to encourage interstate trade. The tariff funds could help improve roads and canals.

> How might a single currency encourage interstate trade?
> _____
> _____

The mainly dirt roads in the United States made travel hard in the early 1800s. The **Cumberland Road** stretched from Cumberland, Maryland, to Wheeling, on the Ohio River in present-day West Virginia. By 1850 its extension reached Illinois.

Construction of the **Erie Canal** started in 1817 and was finished in 1825. Water transportation was often faster, less expensive, and easier than road travel. Using shovels, British, German, and Irish immigrants dug the entire canal by hand. At that time the United States enjoyed an **Era of Good Feelings**. The canal's success was an **incentive** for a canal-building boom across the country.

MISSOURI COMPROMISE

Disagreements between the North and South, known as **sectionalism**, threatened the Union. When Missouri applied to enter the Union, the Union contained 11 free states and 11 slave states. The Senate's balance would favor the South if Missouri entered as a slave state.

Henry Clay persuaded Congress to agree to the **Missouri Compromise**. Missouri entered the Union as a slave state, and Maine entered as a free state. This kept an equal balance in the Senate. Slavery was banned in new territories or states north of Missouri's southern border.

THE ELECTION OF 1824

Senator Andrew Jackson gained the most popular votes but not enough electoral votes to win the election. The House of Representatives chose **John Quincy Adams** as president. Jackson's supporters claimed that Adams had made a "corrupt bargain" with Representative Henry Clay to win. Later, Adams named Clay secretary of state. The election controversy cost Adams support among Americans.

CHALLENGE ACTIVITY

Critical Thinking: Drawing Conclusions Would you support Adams despite the Clay controversy? Why or why not?

> Why were improvements in water transportation so important?
> _____

> How did Henry Clay help Missouri enter the Union?
> _____

> How did Andrew Jackson lose the election of 1824?
> _____

Guided Reading Workbook

DIRECTIONS Match the terms in the first column with their correct definitions from the second column by placing the letter of the correct definition in the space provided before each term.

_____ 1. American System

_____ 2. Era of Good Feelings

_____ 3. Cumberland Road

_____ 4. Erie Canal

_____ 5. sectionalism

_____ 6. Henry Clay

_____ 7. John Quincy Adams

_____ 8. Missouri Compromise

_____ 9. nationalism

a. Henry Clay's plan to improve the U.S. economy

b. U.S. representative who was a strong supporter of national unity

c. allowed goods and people to move between all towns on Lake Erie and New York City

d. settled the conflict surrounding Missouri entering the Union

e. elected president in 1824

f. a sense of pride and devotion to a nation

g. disagreements between different regions

h. the period of prosperity enjoyed by the United States between 1815 and 1825

i. first road built by the federal government

MAIN IDEAS
1. American writers created a new style of literature.
2. A new style of art showcased the beauty of America and its people.
3. American ideals influenced other aspects of culture, including religion and music.
4. Architecture and education were affected by cultural ideals.

Key Terms and People

Washington Irving one of the first American writers to gain international fame

James Fenimore Cooper perhaps the best known of the new American writers

Hudson River school a group of artists whose paintings reflected national pride and an appreciation of the American landscape

Thomas Cole a landscape painter who was a founder of the Hudson River school

George Caleb Bingham an artist whose paintings showed both the American landscape and scenes from people's daily lives

Section Summary
AMERICAN WRITERS

Americans expressed their thoughts and feelings in literature and art. They took spiritual comfort in religion and music. The strengthening national identity was shown in education and architecture. Writers and artists developed familiar American themes and images.

Washington Irving often wrote about American history. He cautioned Americans to learn from the past and prepare for the future. He often used a humorous style of writing called satire. In "Rip Van Winkle," one of his most famous short stories, Irving expresses his idea that Americans must use past lessons to deal with the future.

James Fenimore Cooper wrote about characters who lived on the frontier, including Native Americans. By placing some characters in historical events, he popularized historical fiction.

> **What was Irving's message?**
>
> _____
>
> _____

A NEW STYLE OF ART

The works of Irving and Cooper inspired painters. By the 1830s the **Hudson River school** had appeared. **Thomas Cole** portrayed the American landscape's unique traits. Other painters followed his lead. **George Caleb Bingham** created a painting that shows the rough lives of western traders as well as the landscape. John James Audubon was famous for his paintings of birds.

> How did Bingham depict the West in his paintings?
>
> _____
>
> _____

RELIGION AND MUSIC

Religious revivalism fanned out across America through the early and mid-1800s. Leaders met with large crowds to reawaken religious faith. People sang songs known as spirituals at revival meetings. Spirituals are a kind of folk hymn from both white and African American music traditions. Popular folk music showed the unique views of the nation. "Hunters of Kentucky" honored the Battle of New Orleans. It was used successfully in the presidential campaign of Andrew Jackson in 1828.

> How were spirituals important for religious revival meetings?
>
> _____
>
> _____

ARCHITECTURE AND EDUCATION

In pre-Revolution America, most American architects modeled their designs on the style used in Great Britain. After the Revolution, Thomas Jefferson said that Americans should base their building designs on those of ancient Greece and Rome. Many architects agreed with Jefferson and used Greek and Roman styles.

Americans also found education important. In 1837 Massachusetts set up a state board of education. Other states followed Massachusetts and started their own education systems.

> Why did Jefferson want Americans to change their styles of architecture?
>
> _____
>
> _____

CHALLENGE ACTIVITY

Critical Thinking: Elaborating Would you prefer to be a writer or a landscape artist? Make a choice, and write an essay describing the western American landscape in the 1800s or draw a picture of it.

DIRECTIONS On the line provided before each statement, write **T** if a statement is true and **F** if a statement is false. If the statement is false, write the correct term on the line after each sentence that makes the sentence a true statement.

_____ 1. One of the first American writers to gain international fame was <u>Thomas Cole</u>.

_____

_____ 2. <u>James Fenimore Cooper</u> wrote about the West and the American Indians even though he never saw the American frontier.

_____

_____ 3. A group of artists called the <u>Hudson River school</u> got their name because many of their paintings showed the Hudson River valley.

_____

_____ 4. <u>Washington Irving</u> painted *Fur Traders Descending the Missouri*—a painting that shows the rugged lonely lives of traders in the West.

_____

_____ 5. <u>James Fenimore Cooper</u> was the leader of the Hudson River school.

_____

_____ 6. Historical authors, such as <u>Catharine Maria Sedgwick</u>, created interesting heroines.

_____

_____ 7. <u>James Fenimore Cooper</u> published novels such as *The Last of the Mohicans* and *The Pioneers*.

_____

_____ 8. <u>Washington Irving</u> used a humorous form of writing called satire to warn Americans that they should learn from the past and be cautious about the future.

_____

The Age of Jackson

MAIN IDEAS
1. Democracy expanded in the 1820s as more Americans held the right to vote.
2. Jackson's victory in the election of 1828 marked a change in American politics.

Key Terms and People

nominating conventions public meetings to select a party's presidential and vice presidential candidates

Jacksonian Democracy the democratic expansion that occurred during Jackson's presidency

Democratic Party a party formed by Jackson supporters

John C. Calhoun Jackson's vice presidential running mate

spoils system the practice of rewarding political supporters with government jobs

Martin Van Buren the secretary of the state in Jackson's cabinet

Kitchen Cabinet an informal group of Jackson's trusted advisers that sometimes met in the White House kitchen

Section Summary
EXPANSION OF DEMOCRACY

In the early 1800s state legislatures expanded democracy, giving more people voting rights. However, women and African Americans still had no voting rights in most states.

By 1828 almost all states had changed the system under which state legislatures nominated electors in the electoral college. Now, the people nominated their own electors. Some parties began to hold **nominating conventions**. Broader voting rights and conventions allowed more people to actively participate in politics.

Andrew Jackson entered the political scene as American democracy grew. Historians called the expansion of democracy in this era **Jacksonian Democracy**.

> **Who was left out in the push to give Americans more voting rights?**
> _____
> _____

> **Who supported Jackson for president?**
> _____
> _____

ELECTION OF 1828

Jackson's supporters were mainly farmers, frontier settlers, and southern slaveholders. They believed he would protect the rights of the common people and the slave states. They referred to themselves as Democrats and established the **Democratic Party**. Many supporters of President John Quincy Adams called themselves National Republicans.

The presidential candidates were President Adams and Andrew Jackson in a replay of the 1824 election. Jackson selected South Carolina Senator **John C. Calhoun** as his running mate. The campaign concentrated on personalities. Jackson's campaigners said he was a war hero who was born poor and earned success through hard work. They said that Adams knew nothing about everyday people because his father had been the second U.S. president. Adams's backers said Jackson was too coarse to be president.

> What were some of the key differences between Jackson and Adams?
>
> _____
>
> _____

Jackson and Calhoun won the election. Jackson's supporters described his victory as a triumph for the common people. A crowd of some 20,000 people held a big party on the White House lawn to celebrate. Jackson began the **spoils system**, but he replaced fewer than one-fifth of federal officeholders. One of Jackson's strongest cabinet members was **Martin Van Buren**. Jackson also relied heavily on a trusted group of advisors that was called the **kitchen cabinet**.

> Why might so many people have attended the election party?
>
> _____
>
> _____
>
> _____

CHALLENGE ACTIVITY

Critical Thinking: Analyze Make a chart that includes facts about who supported Jackson and what reasons they had for supporting him.

DIRECTIONS Read each sentence and fill in the blank with the word in the word pair that best completes the sentence.

1. Meetings to select the party's presidential and vice presidential candidates are

   called _____. (Kitchen Cabinets/nominating conventions)

2. Secretary of State _____ was one of President Andrew Jackson's strongest allies in his official cabinet.
   (John C. Calhoun/Martin Van Buren)

3. The South Carolina senator that Andrew Jackson chose to be his vice presidential

   running mate was _____.

   (John C. Calhoun/Martin Van Buren)

4. One group of trusted advisers to President Jackson called the

   _____ was an informal group that sometimes met in the

   White House. (Kitchen Cabinet/nominating convention)

5. A practice known as the _____ was when an elected
   official rewarded some of his supporters with government jobs.
   (spoils system/nominating convention)

DIRECTIONS On the line provided before each statement, write **T** if a statement is true and **F** if a statement is false. If the statement is false, write the correct term on the line after each sentence that makes the sentence a true statement.

_____ 6. The backers of <u>Andrew Jackson</u> were mostly farmers, frontier settlers, and
           southern slaveholders.

           _____

_____ 7. The political party that supported Andrew Jackson was known as the
           <u>Democratic Party</u>.

           _____

_____ 8. <u>John C. Calhoun</u> was elected president of the United States in 1828.

           _____

The Age of Jackson

MAIN IDEAS
1. Regional differences grew during Jackson's presidency.
2. The rights of the states were debated amid arguments about a national tariff.
3. Jackson's attack on the Bank sparked controversy.
4. Jackson's policies led to the Panic of 1837.

Key Terms and People

Tariff of Abominations a tariff with very high rates

states' rights doctrine the belief that state power should be greater than federal power

nullification crisis the dispute over whether states had the right to nullify, or disobey, any federal law with which they disagreed

Daniel Webster a senator from Massachusetts who spoke out against nullification and believed the nation had to stay united

McCulloch v. Maryland the case in which the U.S. Supreme Court ruled that the Second Bank of the United States was constitutional

Whig Party a political group supported by people who opposed Andrew Jackson

Panic of 1837 a financial crisis that led to a severe economic depression

William Henry Harrison a general and the Whig presidential candidate in 1840

Academic Vocabulary

criteria basic requirements

Section Summary

SECTIONAL DIFFERENCES INCREASE

In Andrew Jackson's presidency, people's reaction to almost every policy was based on where they lived and the economy of their region. The North's economy depended on trade and manufacturing. The North supported tariffs, which helped it compete with foreign manufacturers. Southerners marketed a large portion of their crops to foreign countries. Most southerners opposed tariffs, which led to higher prices in manufactured items that they bought. Westerners wanted cheap land.

> **Why did northerners disagree with southerners on the issue of tariffs?**
>
> _____
> _____

Northerners continued to demand high tariffs to guard their new industries from foreign competition. In 1828 Congress passed a law that southerners called the **Tariff of Abominations**. (An abomination is a hateful thing.) The tariff intensified sectional differences.

How did the Tariff of Abominations help industries in the North?

STATES' RIGHTS DEBATE

Early in his career, Vice President John C. Calhoun supported a strong central government. Later on, he argued for states' rights in the **states' rights doctrine**. The debate over states' rights led to the **nullification crisis**. Jackson opposed nullification. Calhoun resigned from office. South Carolina's legislature declared that a new 1832 tariff would not be collected in the state. **Daniel Webster** backed a unified nation. Congress finally agreed to lower the tariffs gradually. South Carolina's leaders agreed to obey the law but still backed the nullification idea.

How did Jackson and Calhoun differ on the debate over states' rights?

JACKSON ATTACKS THE BANK

President Jackson and many southern states questioned the constitutional legality of the Second Bank of the United States. However, in the case *McCulloch v. Maryland*, the Bank was found to be constitutional. Jackson moved most of the Bank's funds to state banks. This action caused inflation.

What happened when the federal bank's funds were moved to state banks?

PANIC OF 1837

The **Whig Party** backed four candidates for president in 1836, and the Democrat, Martin Van Buren, won. When the country experienced the **Panic of 1837**, Van Buren was blamed. In 1840 the Whigs nominated **William Henry Harrison**, who won with an electoral landslide.

Why might voters have chosen Harrison over Van Buren?

CHALLENGE ACTIVITY

Critical Thinking: Summarizing Design a poster that illustrates President Jackson's actions in his two terms. Use captions.

Daniel Webster	Panic of 1837	Whig Party
McCulloch v. *Maryland*	states' rights doctrine	William Henry Harrison
nullification crisis	Tariff of Abominations	

DIRECTIONS Answer each question by writing a sentence that contains at least one word from the word bank.

1. Which Supreme Court case upheld the constitutionality of the Second Bank of the United States?

_____

_____

_____

2. What political party did William Henry Harrison belong to?

_____

_____

_____

3. What rights did John C. Calhoun argue that tariffs violated?

_____

_____

_____

4. What act, passed by Congress in 1828, resulted in increased sectional differences and the nullification crisis?

_____

_____

_____

Section 3

> **MAIN IDEAS**
> 1. The Indian Removal Act authorized the relocation of Native Americans to the West.
> 2. Cherokee resistance to removal led to disagreement between Jackson and the Supreme Court.
> 3. Other Native Americans resisted removal with force.

Key Terms and People

Indian Removal Act the act that authorized the removal of Native Americans who lived east of the Mississippi River

Indian Territory the new homeland for Native Americans, which contained most of present-day Oklahoma

Bureau of Indian Affairs an agency created to oversee the federal policy toward Native Americans

Sequoya a Cherokee who used 86 characters to represent Cherokee syllables to create a written language

Worcester v. Georgia a case in which the U.S. Supreme Court ruled that the state of Georgia had no authority over the Cherokee

Trail of Tears an 800-mile forced march westward in which one-fourth of the 18,000 Cherokee died

Black Hawk a Sauk chief who decided to fight rather than be removed

Osceola Seminole leader who called on Native Americans to resist removal by force

Academic Vocabulary

contemporary existing at the same time

Section Summary

INDIAN REMOVAL ACT

President Andrew Jackson's policies toward Native Americans were controversial. Native Americans had long lived in settlements from Georgia to Mississippi. Jackson and other political leaders wanted this land for American farmers. Jackson pressured Congress to pass the **Indian Removal Act** in 1830. The **Indian Territory** was set aside as a new home for Native Americans.

> Why were Jackson's policies toward Native Americans controversial?
>
> _____
> _____

The **Bureau of Indian Affairs** was established. Indian peoples began to be removed to Indian Territory. They lost their lands east of the Mississippi. On their trips to Indian Territory, many Native Americans died of cold, disease, and starvation. The Cherokee adopted the **contemporary** culture of whites to avoid conflicts. **Sequoya** helped the Cherokee create their own written language.

The Cherokee sued the state when the Georgia militia tried to remove them. In the case *Worcester v. Georgia*, the U.S. Supreme Court ruled in favor of the Cherokee. Georgia ignored the ruling and removed the Cherokee. On the **Trail of Tears**, the Cherokee suffered from heat, cold, and exposure.

> Why was the Indian Territory established?
> _____
> _____

OTHER NATIVE AMERICANS RESIST

Conflicts broke out in Illinois and Florida when some Native Americans decided to resist removal with force. Chief **Black Hawk** led the Sauk of Illinois in raiding settlements and fighting the U.S. Army. The U.S. Army attacked the Sauk as they retreated, and the uprising ended. By 1850 American Indians had been driven from the Illinois region.

In Florida the Seminole also resisted removal. In 1832 some Seminole leaders were forced to sign a treaty that said they would withdraw from Florida in seven years. Any Seminole of African ancestry would be called a runaway slave.

The Seminoles ignored the treaty. **Osceola** led his followers in the Second Seminole War. The Seminole won many battles. Some 1,500 U.S. soldiers died. After spending millions of dollars, U.S. officials gave up.

> How did the Sauk resist removal?
> _____
> _____

> How did the outcome for the Seminole differ from that of other Native Americans?
> _____
> _____

CHALLENGE ACTIVITY

Critical Thinking: Analyzing Write an essay explaining how your view of the Indian Removal Act would compare or contrast with the view of an easterner who wanted to settle on Native American lands.

DIRECTIONS Write two adjectives or descriptive phrases that describe the term.

1. Black Hawk _____

2. Bureau of Indian Affairs _____

3. Indian Removal Act _____

4. Indian Territory _____

5. Osceola _____

6. Sequoya _____

7. *Worcester* v. *Georgia* _____

8. Trail of Tears _____

DIRECTIONS Read each sentence and fill in the blank with the word in the word pair that best completes the sentence.

9. Congress approved the creation of the _____ to oversee the federal policy toward Native Americans.
(Bureau of Indian Affairs/Indian Removal Act)

10. The Cherokee's 800-mile forced march from Georgia to Indian Territory became known as the _____. (Sequoya/Trail of Tears)

11. When U.S. officials ordered the removal of all American Indians from Illinois, Chief _____ decided to fight rather than leave.
(Black Hawk/Sequoya)

Expanding West

MAIN IDEAS
1. During the early 1800s, Americans moved west of the Rocky Mountains to settle and trade.
2. The Mormons traveled west in search of religious freedom.

Key Terms and People

mountain men fur traders and trappers who traveled to the Rocky Mountains and the Pacific Northwest in the early 1800s

John Jacob Astor owner of the American Fur Company who founded the first important settlement in Oregon Country in 1811

Oregon Trail the main route from the Mississippi River to the West Coast in the early 1800s

Santa Fe Trail the route from Independence, Missouri, to Santa Fe, New Mexico

Mormons members of a religious group, formally known as the Church of Jesus Christ of Latter-day Saints, that moved west during the 1830s and 1840s

Brigham Young Mormon leader who chose Utah as the group's new home

Section Summary
AMERICANS MOVE WEST

In the early 1800s trappers and traders known as **mountain men** worked to supply the eastern fashion for fur hats and clothing. **John Jacob Astor,** owner of the American Fur Company, sent mountain men to the Pacific Northwest region that became known as Oregon Country. At this time Oregon Country was inhabited by Native Americans. However, it was claimed by Russia, Spain, Great Britain, and the United States.

In 1811 Astor founded Astoria, which was the first major non-Native American settlement in the region, at the mouth of the Columbia River. After a series of treaties, Oregon Country soon became jointly occupied by Great Britain and the United States. Many Americans began to move to the region, most of them following a challenging and

> **What did mountain men do?**
> _____
> _____

> **Where was the first major non-Native American settlement located?**
> _____
> _____

dangerous route that became known as the **Oregon Trail.** It was common for families to band together and undertake the perilous six-month journey in wagon trains.

Another well-traveled route west, the **Santa Fe Trail,** was used mainly by traders. They loaded wagon trains with cloth and other manufactured goods that could be traded for horses, mules, and silver in the Mexican settlement of Santa Fe.

> **What do you think was the main language spoken in Santa Fe at this time?**
>
> _____
>
> _____

MORMONS TRAVEL WEST

One large group of settlers traveled west in search of religious freedom. Joseph Smith founded the Church of Jesus Christ of Latter-day Saints in 1830 in western New York state. Although church membership grew rapidly, the converts, known as **Mormons,** were dogged by local hostility. To protect his growing community from persecution, Smith led his followers to a series of settlements in Ohio, Missouri, and Illinois.

When Smith was murdered by an anti-Mormon mob in 1844, **Brigham Young** led the Mormons to a desert valley near the Great Salt Lake in what is now Utah. There the Mormons planned and built Salt Lake City and settled in the area. By December 1860 the Mormon population of Utah stood at about 40,000.

> **Why did Mormon leaders create a series of settlements?**
>
> _____
>
> _____

CHALLENGE ACTIVITY

Critical Thinking: Drawing Inferences Make a list of supplies that a family of four would need to make a six-month journey by wagon train through the American West during the 1830s.

DIRECTIONS Look at each set of three vocabulary terms following each number. On the line provided, write the letter of the term that does not relate to the other terms.

_____ 1. a. mountain men   _____ 2. a. Brigham Young
          b. Brigham Young   b. Mormons
          c. John Jacob Astor   c. mountain men

DIRECTIONS Write two adjectives or descriptive phrases that describe the term given.

3. Brigham Young _____

4. John Jacob Astor _____

5. Mormons _____

6. mountain men _____

7. Oregon Trail _____

DIRECTIONS On the line provided before each statement, write **T** if a statement is true and **F** if a statement is false. If the statement is false, write the correct term on the line after each sentence that makes the sentence a true statement.

_____ 8. Joseph Smith founded the Church of Jesus Christ of Latter-day Saints, whose members became known as <u>mountain men</u>.

_____

_____ 9. The American Fur Company, which was owned by <u>Brigham Young</u>, was one of the largest businesses that bought furs from trappers.

_____

_____ 10. Fur traders and trappers who traveled to the Rocky Mountains and Pacific Northwest were called <u>Mormons</u>.

_____

Expanding West

MAIN IDEAS
1. Many American settlers moved to Texas after Mexico achieved independence from Spain.
2. Texans revolted against Mexican rule and established an independent nation.

Key Terms and People

Father Miguel Hidalgo y Costilla priest who led the first major Mexican revolt against Spanish rule in 1810

empresarios agents of the Mexican republic hired to bring settlers to Texas

Stephen F. Austin empresario who established the first American colony in Texas

Antonio López de Santa Anna Mexican leader who came to power in 1830 and suspended Mexico's constitution

Alamo an old mission in San Antonio occupied by Texan revolutionary forces in 1836

Battle of San Jacinto decisive victory that gave Texas independence from Mexico

Academic Vocabulary

explicit fully revealed without vagueness

Section Summary

AMERICAN SETTLERS MOVE TO TEXAS

In the early 1800s, the region we now know as the American Southwest was part of Mexico, which in turn was part of the vast Spanish empire in the Americas. Mexico struggled against Spanish rule. A revolt led by **Father Miguel Hidalgo y Costilla** in 1810 failed, but the rebellion he started grew. In 1821 Mexico became independent.

In order to establish control of Texas, the new Mexican republic hired agents known as **empresarios** to bring settlers there. One of these, **Stephen F. Austin,** selected a site on the lower Colorado River and settled 300 families, mostly from the southern states. These settlers often

> During the early 1800s, what empire did California and Texas belong to?
>
> _____
>
> _____

> From what region of the United States did most settlers come to Texas?
>
> _____
>
> _____

explicity ignored Mexican laws, including Mexico's law forbidding slavery.

Tension grew between Mexico's central government and the American settlers. Colonists were angry when **Antonio López de Santa Anna** came to power in 1830 and suspended Mexico's constitution. Austin was imprisoned for a year and a half. When he returned to Texas, he began urging Texans to rebel against Mexico.

> Underline the sentence that helps explain why tension grew between the central Mexican government and the American settlers in Texas.

TEXANS REVOLT AGAINST MEXICO

Hostilities began with a battle at Gonzalez in 1835. Santa Anna inflicted two brutal defeats on the Texans at the **Alamo** and Goliad. Within a month, however, Texas forces under Sam Houston had won a decisive victory over Santa Anna at the **Battle of San Jacinto.** Santa Anna signed a treaty giving Texas its independence.

Most people in the new Republic of Texas hoped that Texas would join the United States. However, U.S. President Andrew Jackson was concerned about two factors. He was worried that admitting Texas as a slave state would upset the fragile balance between free and slave states in the Union. Also, Jackson feared that annexing Texas might lead to a war with Mexico.

As the annexation of Texas was delayed, more American settlers came from nearby southern states, often bringing slaves with them to work the land and to grow cotton. Tensions between Mexico and Texas remained high. After a few unsettled years, Texas President Sam Houston signed a peace treaty with Mexico in 1844.

> What did many American settlers bring with them to Texas?
>
> _____
>
> _____

CHALLENGE ACTIVITY

Critical Thinking: Evaluation Take sides in a debate as to whether Texas should join the United States or remain an independent nation. Write an explicit defense of your position.

Alamo	Stephen F. Austin	Battle of San Jacinto
empresarios	Father Miguel Hidalgo y Costilla	Republic of Texas
	Antonio López de Santa Anna	

DIRECTIONS Write two adjectives or descriptive phrases that describe
the term given.

1. empresarios _____

2. Stephen F. Austin _____

3. Antonio López de Santa Anna _____

4. Alamo _____

5. Battle of San Jacinto _____

DIRECTIONS Read each sentence and fill in the blank with the word
in the word pair that best completes the sentence.

6. In 1820 _____ led a rebellion of about 80,000 poor
   American Indians and mestizos hoping to win Mexico's independence from
   Spain. (Antonio López de Santa Anna/Father Miguel Hidalgo y Costilla)

7. _____ was one of the empresarios who brought settlers to
   Texas. (Stephen F. Austin/Sam Houston)

8. Sam Houston's Texas army defeated _____ at the

   _____. (Antonio López de Santa Anna/Father Miguel

   Hidalgo y Costilla); (Alamo/Battle of San Jacinto)

9. The independent nation of Texas was called the _____
   (Alamo/Republic of Texas)

Name _____ · Class _____ Date _____

Expanding West

 MAIN IDEAS
1. Many Americans believed that the nation had a manifest destiny to claim new lands in the West.
2. As a result of the Mexican-American War, the United States added territory in the Southwest.
3. American settlement in the Mexican Cession produced conflict and a blending of cultures.

Key Terms and People

manifest destiny belief that America's fate was to conquer land all the way to the Pacific Ocean

James K. Polk U.S. president, elected in 1844, whose administration annexed both Texas and Oregon

vaqueros cowboys

Californios Spanish colonists and their descendents living in California

Bear Flag Revolt rebellion of American settlers against the Californios in 1846

Treaty of Guadalupe Hidalgo 1848 peace treaty between Mexico and the United States

Gadsden Purchase purchase from Mexico of the southern parts of present-day New Mexico and Arizona in 1853

Academic Vocabulary

elements a basic part of an individual's surroundings

Section Summary

MANIFEST DESTINY

The idea of manifest destiny loomed large in the election of 1844. The new president, **James K. Polk,** promised to annex both Texas and Oregon.

In 1846 Britain and the United States signed a treaty that gave the United States all Oregon land south of the 49th parallel. This treaty drew the present-day border between the United States and Canada. In 1845 the congresses of both the Republic of Texas and the United States approved annexation of Texas.

> How did the boundaries of the United States change during the 1840s?
>
> _____
>
> _____

After winning independence from Spain in 1821, Mexico began changing old policies set by Spain. Mission lands were broken up into vast ranches. *Vaqueros* managed the herds of cattle and sheep.Settlers, known as **Californios,** felt little connection to their faraway government in Mexico. American settlers also began coming to California and calling for independence from Mexico.

> **How might Californios have viewed the arrival of large numbers of American settlers?**
>
> _____
>
> _____
>
> _____
>
> _____

MEXICAN-AMERICAN WAR

Since the Texas Revolution the border between Mexico and Texas had been in dispute. Mexico claimed the border lay along the Nueces River while the United States claimed the Rio Grande as the border. In 1845 President Polk sent troops to the Rio Grande. When Mexican soldiers attacked them, Congress declared war on Mexico. Although many Americans thought the war was unjustified, U.S. troops pushed into Mexico, going from victory to victory until they finally captured Mexico City. A successful revolt against the Californios in Sonoma, known as the **Bear Flag Revolt,** proclaimed California to be an independent nation.

> **Some Americans at the time thought President Polk provoked the Mexican attack by stationing soldiers on the Rio Grande. Do you agree? Explain your answer.**
>
> _____
>
> _____

AMERICAN SETTLEMENT IN THE MEXICAN CESSION

The **Treaty of Guadalupe Hidalgo,** which ended the Mexican War in 1848, increased the land area of the United States by almost 25 percent. A few years later, in 1853, the **Gadsden Purchase** fixed the con-tinental boundaries of the United States.

As American settlers flooded the Southwest, the **elements** of life changed. Cultural encounters often led to conflict and violence. New settlers usually ignored Mexican legal ideas, such as community property and water rights. However, traditional knowledge and customs gradually shaped local economies, and new and mutually beneficial trade patterns began to emerge.

> **Why is the issue of water rights much more serious in the West than it is in the East?**
>
> _____
>
> _____
>
> _____

CHALLENGE ACTIVITY

Critical Thinking: Identify Cause and Effect

Write a law regulating water rights.

Guided Reading Workbook

DIRECTIONS Read each sentence and fill in the blank with the word
in the word pair that best completes the sentence.

1. The Democratic Party chose former Tennessee governor

   _____ as its presidential candidate in the election of 1844.

   (James K. Polk/Henry Clay)

2. The _____ was negotiated with Mexico so that the United

   States government would pay Mexico for the southern parts of what are now

   Arizona and New Mexico. (Gadsden Purchase/Bear Flag Revolt)

3. The growth of the United States to the Pacific Ocean was called

   _____ (Californios/manifest destiny)

4. The Mexican-American War ended with the signing of the

   _____ (manifest destiny/Treaty of Guadalupe Hidalgo)

5. Spanish colonists in California were known as _____

   (Californios/manifest destiny)

6. This rebellion was called the _____ because of the flag

   that was created to represent the nation of California.

   (Bear Flag Revolt/Gadsden Purchase)

7. _____ was elected president of the United States in 1844.

   (Henry Clay/James K. Polk)

8. The _____ finally fixed the continental boundaries of the

   United States. (Bear Flag Revolt/Gadsden Purchase)

9. General _____ led U.S. troops against Mexico.

   (Zachary Taylor/James K. Polk)

10. In the_____, Mexico turned over to the United States land

    that included the present-day states of California, Nevada, and Utah, and parts of

    Arizona, New Mexico, Colorado, and Wyoming. (Bear Flag Revolt/Mexican

    Cession)

Expanding West

MAIN IDEAS
1. The discovery of gold brought settlers to California.
2. The gold rush had a lasting impact on California's population and economy.

Key Terms and People

John Sutter Swiss immigrant who started the first Anglo-Californian colony in 1839

Donner party a group of western travelers who were trapped crossing the Sierra Nevada Mountains in the winter of 1846 –47

forty-niners gold-seeking migrants who traveled to California in 1849

prospect search for gold

placer miners miners who used pans or other devices to wash gold nuggets from loose rock or gravel

Section Summary

DISCOVERY OF GOLD BRINGS SETTLERS

Before 1840 few Americans settled in California, although there was considerable trade between merchants from Mexico and the United States. However, after Mexico allowed **John Sutter** to establish a colony in 1839, American settlers began arriving in greater numbers. In a tragic incident, heavy snows in the Sierra Nevada Mountains trapped a group of travelers known as the **Donner party.** Half of the travelers either froze or starved to death.

When gold was discovered at Sutter's Mill in 1848, the news spread across the country. During 1849 about 80,000 **forty-niners** came to California hoping to strike it rich. Most of them arrived in the small port town of San Francisco. Within a year, the population of San Francisco grew from around 800 to more than 25,000.

Mining methods varied by the time of year and the location of the claim. **Placer miners** would

What country was California part of in 1840?
_____
_____

prospect by using pans or other devices to wash gold nuggets out of the loose rock and gravel. Richer miners established companies to dig shafts and tunnels. Many individual success stories inspired prospectors. However, the good luck that made some miners wealthy never came to thousands of gold seekers. Most of them found little except misery and debt.

Mining camps sprang up wherever enough people gathered to look for gold. Among the gold seekers were thousands of immigrants from Mexico, China, Europe, and South America. Many found that they could earn a living by supplying miners with basic services like cooking, washing clothes, operating boardinghouses, or even pro-viding legal services. Biddy Mason and her family, slaves brought to California by a forty-niner from Georgia, gained their freedom and managed to buy some land near the village of Los Angeles. Soon Mason became one of the weathiest landowners in California.

Would mining experience have helped the average forty-niner? Explain your answer.
_____
_____
_____
_____

Who had more "job security," the miners or the service providers? Why?
_____
_____
_____
_____

IMPACT ON CALIFORNIA

The forty-niners brought a population explosion and an economic boom to California. It became the 31st state of the Union in 1850. As the gold rush faded, many Californians took to farming and ranching. However, California remained isolated from the rest of the country until the transcontinental railroad was completed in 1869.

What consequence of the gold rush made California eligible for statehood?
_____
_____

CHALLENGE ACTIVITY

Critical Thinking: Drawing Inferences Design and write a brochure inviting easterners to come to Sutter's colony in California and start a new life.

Donner party	forty-niners	Biddy Mason	prospect
Levi Strauss	John Sutter	Sutter's Mill	

DIRECTIONS Write two adjectives or descriptive phrases that describe the term given.

1. forty-niners _____

2. prospect _____

3. Biddy Mason _____

DIRECTIONS On the line provided before each statement, write **T** if a statement is true and **F** if a statement is false. If the statement is false, write the correct term on the line after each sentence that makes the sentence a true statement.

_____ 4. <u>Levi Strauss</u> arrived in California as a slave, but gained freedom and became one of the wealthiest landowners in California, a community leader, and a well-known supporter of charities.

_____

_____ 5. Swiss immigrant <u>John Sutter</u> was given permission by Mexican officials to start a colony in California.

_____

_____ 6. The <u>Donner party</u> was a group of western travelers that became lost in the Sierra Nevada mountains.

_____

_____ 7. When it was learned that gold was discovered near <u>Biddy Mason</u>, the California gold rush began.

_____

Section 1

MAIN IDEAS
1. The invention of new machines in Great Britain led to the beginning of the Industrial Revolution.
2. The development of new machines and processes brought the Industrial Revolution to the United States.
3. Despite a slow start in manufacturing, the United States made rapid improvements during the War of 1812.

Key Terms and People

Industrial Revolution a period of rapid growth in the use of machines in manufacturing and production

textiles cloth items

Richard Arkwright an inventor who patented a large spinning machine, called the water frame, that ran on water power and created dozens of cotton threads at once

Samuel Slater a skilled British mechanic who could build the new textile machines

technology the tools used to produce items or to do work

Eli Whitney an inventor with an idea for mass-producing guns

interchangeable parts pieces that are exactly the same

mass production the efficient production of large numbers of identical goods

Academic Vocabulary

efficient productive and not wasteful

Section Summary
THE INDUSTRIAL REVOLUTION

In the early 1700s, most people in the United States and Europe made a living by farming. Female family members often used hand tools to make cloth for families. The sale of extra cloth earned money. Skilled workers such as blacksmiths set up shops to earn money by manufacturing goods by hand.

The **Industrial Revolution** would completely change that way of life. By the mid-1700s, cities and populations had grown. Demand increased for **efficient** and faster ways to make items.

> In what way were goods made in the early 1700s?
> _____
> _____
> _____

Textiles provided the first breakthrough. **Richard Arkwright** invented a machine that lowered the cost of cotton cloth and raised production speed. The machine was large and needed a power source. Most textile mills were built near streams to use running water for power.

In what way did Arkwright's machine make history?
_____
_____

NEW MACHINES AND PROCESSES

Samuel Slater knew how to build machines that were used in Britain to make cloth more efficiently. He emigrated to the United States, and with Moses Brown opened a mill in Pawtucket, Rhode Island. The mill made cotton thread by machine. It was a success. Most mills were in the northeast, the region with many rivers and streams for power.

What information did Slater bring with him to the United States?
_____
_____

A MANUFACURING BREAKTHROUGH

In the 1790s U.S. gun makers could not produce muskets quickly enough to satisfy the government's demand. Better **technology** was needed. **Eli Whitney** had the idea of manufacturing using **interchangeable parts**. Whitney assembled muskets for President Adams. His idea worked. **Mass production** was soon used in factories making interchangeable parts.

What was Whitney's revolutionary idea?
_____
_____
_____

MANUFACTURING GROWS SLOWLY

U.S. manufacturing spread slowly. People who could buy good farmland would not work for low factory wages. British goods were cheaper than American goods. However, during the War of 1812 many Americans learned that they had relied on foreign goods too much. In 1815 the war ended and free trade returned. Business people were eager to lead the nation into a time of industrial growth.

Why had Americans relied on foreign goods too much?
_____
_____

CHALLENGE ACTIVITY

Critical Thinking: Rating In comparing the three inventors in Section 1, rate them from 1 to 3. Defend your rating order in a brief essay.

Eli Whitney	Industrial Revolution	interchangeable parts
mass production	Richard Arkwright	Samuel Slater
technology	textiles	

DIRECTIONS Read each sentence and fill in the blank with the word in the word pair that best completes the sentence.

1. The _____ was a period of rapid growth in the use of machines in manufacturing and production.
(interchangeable parts/Industrial Revolution)

2. The efficient production of large numbers of identical goods is called
_____. (mass production/Industrial Revolution)

3. Products with _____ are made from pieces that are exactly the same. (interchangeable parts/textiles)

4. People began looking for ways to use machines to make items quickly and
efficiently, thus leading to the _____.
(textiles/Industrial Revolution)

5. Englishman _____ invented a large spinning machine, called
the water frame, that ran on water power. (Samuel Slater/Richard Arkwright)

6. _____ was a skilled British mechanic who knew how to
build the new textile machines. (Samuel Slater/Richard Arkwright)

7. The tools used to produce items or to do work are called
_____. (textiles/technology)

8. Inventor _____ came up with the idea of using
interchangeable parts. (Samuel Slater/Eli Whitney)

9. The first important breakthrough of the Industrial Revolution took place in how
_____, or cloth items, were made. (textiles/technology)

MAIN IDEAS
1. The spread of mills in the Northeast changed workers' lives.
2. The Lowell system revolutionized the textile industry in the Northeast.
3. Workers organized to reform working conditions

Key Terms and People

Rhode Island system Samuel Slater's strategy of hiring families and dividing factory work into simple tasks

Francis Cabot Lowell a New England businessman who built a loom that could both weave thread and spin cloth in the same mill

Lowell system Lowell's practice of hiring young unmarried women to work in his mills

trade unions groups of skilled workers that tried to improve members' pay and working conditions

strikes union workers' refusal to work until their employers met their demands

Sarah G. Bagley a mill worker who founded the Lowell Female Labor Reform Association

Academic Vocabulary

concrete specific, real

Section Summary
MILLS CHANGE WORKERS' LIVES

Samuel Slater had difficulty hiring enough people to work in his mills. Young male apprentices often left because their work was boring. Slater began hiring entire families to move to Pawtucket.

Slater constructed housing for the workers. He paid workers in credit at the company store rather than paying them cash. This way Slater could reinvest money in his business. Children usually earned in one week what an adult was paid for one day's work. Slater's method was known as the **Rhode Island system**. Many northeastern mill owners imitated Slater's system.

> **How much did child workers earn in factories?**
>
> _____
>
> _____

THE LOWELL SYSTEM

Francis Cabot Lowell developed a different approach called the **Lowell system**. It transformed the Northeast's textile industry. With the aid of a company, Lowell built mills in Waltham and Lowell, both in Massachusetts. The factories were clean, and the workers' boardinghouses were neat.

Many young women, called Lowell girls, journeyed from across New England to earn money instead of earning nothing on the family farm. The Lowell girls were encouraged to take classes and join clubs. However, they worked 12- to 14-hour days, and cotton dust caused health problems for them.

> **Name one advantage and one disadvantage of Lowell mill work.**
> _____
> _____
> _____

WORKERS ORGANIZE

Factory workers' wages went down as people competed for jobs. Immigrants also competed for jobs. The Panic of 1837 led to unemployment for many. Skilled workers started **trade unions** for protection. Sometimes union members held **strikes**. But most strikes were not very successful.

Sarah G. Bagley battled for the workers. She was the first highly ranked woman in America's labor movement. In 1840 President Martin Van Buren had given a 10-hour workday to many federal employees. Bagley wanted the 10-hour workday for all workers.

The Unions won some **concrete** legal victories. Some states passed 10-hour workday laws. But companies often found ways to get around them. Other states did not pass the 10-hour workday laws. Union supporters kept fighting for improved working conditions during the 1800s.

> **Why did workers' pay decrease?**
> _____
> _____

> **What did workers achieve in the mid-1800s?**
> _____
> _____

CHALLENGE ACTIVITY

Critical Thinking: Contrasting Write a letter to the editor contrasting the lives of workers in Slater's mills and Lowell's mills.

| Sarah G. Bagley | Francis Cabot Lowell | Lowell system |
| Rhode Island system | strikes | trade unions |

DIRECTIONS On the line provided before each statement, write **T** if a statement is true and **F** if a statement is false. If the statement is false, write the correct term on the line after each sentence that makes the sentence a true statement.

_____ 1. The Lowell system included practices such as hiring young unmarried women from local farms to work in the textile mill.

_____

_____ 2. Sometimes union members staged protests called trade unions.

_____

_____ 3. The Lowell system was Samuel Slater's strategy of hiring families and dividing factory work into simple tasks.

_____

_____ 4. One of the strongest voices in the union movement belonged to Sarah G. Bagley, who founded the Lowell Female Labor Reform Association.

_____

_____ 5. Francis Cabot Lowell was a businessman from New England whose mills used a loom that could both spin thread and weave cloth in the same mill.

_____

_____ 6. Groups that tried to improve pay and working conditions for their members were called strikes.

_____

_____ 7. Mill owners advertised for "Men with growing families wanted" in support of the Lowell system.

_____

_____ 8. Workers on strike refuse to work until their employers meet their demands.

_____

MAIN IDEAS
1. The Transportation Revolution affected trade and daily life.
2. The steamboat was one of the first developments of the Transportation Revolution.
3. Railroads were a vital part of the Transportation Revolution.
4. The Transportation Revolution brought many changes to American life and industry.

Key Terms and People

Transportation Revolution a period of rapid growth in the speed and convenience of travel

Robert Fulton an American who had the first full-time commercial steamboat in the United States

Clermont a steamboat that could travel up the Hudson River with no trouble

Gibbons v. *Ogden* the first U.S. Supreme Court ruling on commerce between states

Peter Cooper an American who built the *Tom Thumb*, a small steam train with great power and speed

Section Summary

TRADE AND DAILY LIFE

Along with the Industrial Revolution, the **Transportation Revolution** changed life and boosted the economy in the 1800s by speeding travel and decreasing cost of shipping goods. People and information began traveling at much higher speeds. New towns and businesses sprang up with improved communication, travel, and trade. The steamboat and the railroad, new kinds of transportation, quickened the pace of American life.

STEAMBOATS

In the late 1700s American and European inventors advanced steam-powered boats. **Robert Fulton** tested the *Clermont* in the United States. The successful test helped launch the steamboat era.

> Why did information begin traveling at higher speeds?
>
> _____
>
> _____
>
> _____

> In what way might the pace of American life have increased?
>
> _____
>
> _____
>
> _____

Steamboats cut months off the time needed to travel from one place to another. They made trips up rivers cheaper and easier. Shipping goods from East to West, West to East, or overseas also was easier.

Sometimes the changes in transportation led to legal conflicts. In a landmark case, ***Gibbons* v. *Ogden***, the court ruled that federal shipping laws overruled state shipping laws.

> **How did steamboats affect shipping?**
> _____
> _____
> _____

AMERICAN RAILROADS

In 1830 **Peter Cooper** built the *Tom Thumb*, a small but fast train. Excitement over rail travel grew in the mid-1800s. By 1860 about 30,000 miles of railroad tracks joined nearly every major eastern U.S. city. Trains took goods to faraway markets. Train travel averaged about 20 miles per hour and could be dangerous because of fires and derailment. But the dangers did not discourage travelers who wanted to go places faster.

> **Circle the sentence that explains why travelers put up with the dangers of railroad travel.**

TRANSPORTATION REVOLUTION BRINGS CHANGES

Trains brought new residents and raw materials for industry to cities, spurring growth. Coal replaced wood as a source of fuel because of its greater efficiency. That led to growth in the mining industry. Steel was used for railroad tracks, so the demand for steel increased. Railroad transportation also helped logging expand because wood was needed to build new houses in the growing cities. Chicago, on Lake Michigan, became a hub for national transportation.

> **What helped the steel industry?**
> _____
> _____

CHALLENGE ACTIVITY

Critical Thinking: Designing Design a four-page brochure advertising the wonders of travel by steamboat or train.

DIRECTIONS Write two adjectives or descriptive phrases that describe the term.

1. *Clermont* _____

2. *Gibbons* v. *Ogden* _____

3. Peter Cooper _____

4. Robert Fulton _____

5. Transportation Revolution _____

DIRECTIONS Look at each set of four vocabulary terms following each number. On the line provided, write the letter of the term that does not relate to the others.

_____ 6. a. *Clermont*   b. Robert Fulton   c. *Tom Thumb*   d. steamboat

_____ 7. a. *Tom Thumb*   b. steamboat   c. Peter Cooper   d. locomotive

_____ 8. a. coal   b. steel   c. fuel   d. wood

DIRECTIONS Read each sentence and fill in the blank with the word in the word pair that best completes the sentence.

9. The Supreme Court ruled in the case of _____ that federal law overruled state law. (*Tom Thumb*/*Gibbons* v. *Ogden*)

10. During the Transportation Revolution, _____ replaced wood as the main source of power. (steel/coal)

11. _____ designed the first full-sized commercial steamboat, called the _____, in the United States.

(Peter Cooper/Robert Fulton); (*Clermont*/*Tom Thumb*)

12. The locomotive _____, built by _____, started an interest in railroads in the United States.
(*Clermont*/*Tom Thumb*); (Peter Cooper/Robert Fulton)

13. A period of rapid growth in the speed and convenience of travel is called the

_____. (Transportation Revolution/Industrial Revolution)

MAIN IDEAS

1. The telegraph made swift communication possible from coast to coast.
2. With the shift to steam power, businesses built factories closer to cities and transportation centers.
3. Improved farm equipment and other labor-saving devices made life easier for many Americans.
4. New inventions changed lives in American homes.

Key Terms and People

Samuel F. B. Morse the inventor of the telegraph

telegraph a device that could send information over wires across great distances

Morse code a system in which dots and dashes are used to stand for each letter of the alphabet

John Deere a blacksmith who first used the steel plow design

Cyrus McCormick the developer of a new harvesting machine called a mechanical reaper

Isaac Singer an inventor who made improvements in the design of the sewing machine

Section Summary

TELEGRAPH SPEEDS COMMUNICATION

Samuel F. B. Morse invented the **telegraph** in 1832. Morse used the work of two other scientists in making this practical machine. Telegraphs carry pulses, or surges, of electric current over wires. The operator touches a bar, called a telegraph key, that sets the length of each pulse. At the wire's other end, the pulses change into clicks. A short click is a dot; a long click is a dash.

Morse's assistant, Alfred Lewis Vail, developed the **Morse code**. Some people did not think Morse could actually read messages sent across long distances. But during the 1844 Democratic Convention in Baltimore, Maryland, a telegraph wired news of a nomination to politicians who were

> **What was the invention of the telegraph based on?**
>
> _____
>
> _____

> **Did everyone accept the telegraph's power at first?**
>
> _____
>
> _____

in Washington. Soon telegraphs were relaying messages for businesses, the government, newspapers, and private citizens. The economy grew more united as people used telegraph lines to conduct business with partners across the country.

Why did telegraph messages become so widely used?
_____
_____
_____

STEAM POWERED FACTORIES

Most factories, operating on water power at first, had to be built near water. With the use of steam engines, factories could be built almost anywhere. Still, most were in the Northeast. By 1860 New England had as many factories as all of the South had. Many new factories were near cities and transportation centers, giving them better access to workers. In addition, by the 1840s new machinery could produce interchangeable parts.

Why could newer factories be built almost anywhere?
_____
_____
_____

IMPROVED FARM EQUIPMENT

John Deere was selling 1,000 steel plows a year by 1846. **Cyrus McCormick** mass-produced his reapers in a large Chicago factory. His company advertised, provided service, and let customers buy on credit. The plow and the reaper allowed Midwestern farmers to harvest huge wheat fields.

Circle the sentence that explains what new methods McCormick used to persuade people to buy his reapers.

CHANGING LIFE AT HOME

The sewing machine was among the American inventions that made home life easier. **Isaac Singer** modified the sewing machine and worked hard to sell his product. Prices of many household items had decreased, giving many more people the ability to afford them.

Why did the purchase of many household items increase?
_____
_____
_____

CHALLENGE ACTIVITY

Critical Thinking: Evaluating Write a brief essay explaining which invention mentioned in this section made the biggest change in people's lives.

John Deere	Cyrus McCormick	Samuel F. B. Morse
Morse code	Isaac Singer	telegraph

DIRECTIONS Match the names in the first column with the invention or development with which they are associated from the second column by placing the letter of the correct definition in the space provided before each term.

_____ 1. Samuel F. B. Morse

_____ 2. John Deere

_____ 3. Isaac Singer

_____ 4. Cyrus McCormick

_____ 5. Alfred Lewis Vail

_____ 6. Elias Howe

a. developed the mechanical reaper

b. improved and marketed the sewing machine

c. developed Morse code

d. perfected the telegraph

e. invented the sewing machine

f. designed a steel plow

DIRECTIONS Choose five of the vocabulary words from the word list. Use these words to write a summary of what you learned in the section.

_____

_____

_____

_____

_____

_____

_____

_____

_____

_____

MAIN IDEAS
1. The invention of the cotton gin revived the economy of the South.
2. The cotton gin created a cotton boom in which farmers grew little else.
3. Some people encouraged southerners to focus on other crops and industries.

Key Terms and People

cotton gin machine that separates cotton from its seeds

planters large-scale farmers who owned more than 20 slaves

cotton belt nickname for the region that grew most of the country's cotton crop

factors crop brokers who arranged transportation of goods aboard trading ships

Tredegar Iron Works in its day, the only large southern factory that made iron products

Academic Vocabulary

primary main, most important

Section Summary

REVIVING THE SOUTH'S ECONOMY

After the American Revolution, the use of slaves began to decline. Because crop prices fell, farmers planted less, so they needed less slave labor.

Cotton was not a new crop to the southern states. However, few farmers planted much, for the shortstaple cotton that grew well there was very hard to separate from its seeds. Northerner Eli Whitney changed that when he invented the **cotton gin**.

This hand-cranked cylinder easily pulled cotton and seeds apart. With the cotton gin, cotton crops became profitable. A cotton gin could clean as much cotton as planters could plant and their slaves could pick. A **planter** was a large-scale farmer who owned more than 20 slaves.

> Why was it difficult to harvest cotton before the invention of the cotton gin?
> _____
> _____

THE COTTON BOOM

For southern farmers cotton had many advantages over other crops. Unlike food products cotton could be stored for long periods of time. Plus its lightness made it fairly inexpensive to transport. As a result, the cotton-supported slave trade grew, even as Congress worked to limit slavery in the nation.

Most of the country's cotton was produced in the **cotton belt**, which stretched from South Carolina to Texas. Without transportation systems such as roads and canals, southern farmers relied on rivers to move their cotton. When the cotton reached a port, the farmers sold their cotton to merchants who then contacted **factors** to arrange transportation for the cotton aboard trading ships.

> **What were the advantages of cotton compared to other crops?**
> _____
> _____

> **Why were the region's rivers especially important to southern farmers?**
> _____
> _____

OTHER CROPS AND INDUSTRIES

Scientific agriculture, or the use of scientific methods to improve farming, encouraged southern farmers to rotate the kinds of crops they planted. The **primary** food crop of the South was corn, but farmers also grew rice, sugarcane, wheat, tobacco, hemp, and flax. Some southerners encouraged the growth of industry so that the South would be less reliant on goods from the North and other countries. More variety in crops and industries would help the South avoid some of the federal government's tariff policies. As a result, some industries, such as the **Tredegar Iron Works**, also flourished. Still, most of the South focused on farming.

> **Circle the definition of scientific agriculture.**

CHALLENGE ACTIVITY

Critical Thinking: Write to Explain What if a new fiber was discovered that replaced cotton in clothing? What effect would this development have on cotton planters? Write a paragraph explaining how falling cotton prices might lead to less demand for farm workers.

DIRECTIONS Look at each set of four vocabulary terms. On the line provided, write the letter of the term that does not relate to the others.

_____ 1. a. Eli Whitney　　　　　　　_____ 4. a. Joseph R. Anderson
　　　　 b. cotton gin　　　　　　　　　　　　 b. cotton belt
　　　　 c. Joseph R. Anderson　　　　　　　　 c. planters
　　　　 d. planters　　　　　　　　　　　　　 d. cotton gin

_____ 2. a. Joseph R. Anderson　　　 _____ 5. a. factors
　　　　 b. planters　　　　　　　　　　　　　 b. Eli Whitney
　　　　 c. Tredegar Iron Works　　　　　　　　 c. Tredegar Iron Works
　　　　 d. industry　　　　　　　　　　　　　 d. scientific agriculture

_____ 3. a. scientific agriculture
　　　　 b. cotton belt
　　　　 c. factors
　　　　 d. Tredegar Iron Works

DIRECTIONS Read each sentence and fill in the blank with the word in the word pair that best completes the sentence.

6. The _____ was a simple device that used a hand-cranked cylinder with wire teeth to pull cotton fibers apart from the seeds. (cotton gin/cotton belt)

7. _____ were large-scale farmers who held more than 20 slaves. (planters/factors)

8. The region that stretched from South Carolina to Texas became known as the

_____, because it was the area that grew most of the

country's cotton. (cotton gin/cotton belt)

9. The _____ in Richmond, Virginia, produced bridge materials, cannons, steam engines, and other products. (Eli Whitney/Tredegar Iron Works)

10. Crop brokers called _____ managed the cotton trade in port cities. (planters/factors)

Section 2

MAIN IDEAS
1. Southern society and culture consisted of four main groups.
2. Free African Americans in the South faced a great deal of discrimination.

Key Terms and People

yeomen owners of small farms

Section Summary

SOUTHERN SOCIETY AND CULTURE

Only about one-third of all southerners owned slaves. Far fewer were actually wealthy planters. However, those few planters were among the most influential southern citizens, and many were political leaders. The economy of the South was dependent on agriculture, and most agricultural production relied on slave plantations.

On the vast plantations, the planter ran the farm business. A wealthy planter would have overseers to help him. The planter's wife ran the household, which included many house slaves. She also was in charge of important social events such as dances and dinners.

Most southern farmers were yeomen. **Yeomen** owned small farms averaging about 100 acres, and often they worked side by side with the few slaves they might own.

Many white southerners were poor. They owned no slaves at all. Often they lived on land that could not grow crops. These farmers were at the bottom of the economic ladder.

Religion was central to southern life. One reason was its social impact. Often farm families only saw their neighbors at church functions. Some southerners also believed that Christianity justified slavery—a belief not shared by Christians in the North.

How was a yeoman different from a planter?
_____
_____
_____

Why was religion central to southern life?
_____
_____

The economy of the South also depended on the businesses conducted in its busy cities. As in northern cities, southern cities provided many services to residents, including water systems and street maintenance. Southern cities used slave labor, too. Businesses either owned slaves or hired them out from nearby planters.

How were southern cities like northern cities?
_____
_____
_____

FREE AFRICAN AMERICANS AND DISCRIMINATION

Not all African Americans were slaves. Some were free. Some had been born free. Others had bought their freedom from their slave owners or had run away. About half of these free African Americans lived in the South.

Circle the sentence describing how many of free African Americans lived in the South.

The presence of free African Americans concerned some white southerners. They worried that those who were free would incite those who were enslaved to rise up against their owners. As a result, southern cities and states passed laws aimed at limiting the rights of these free African Americans.

According to many southerners, how did free African Americans threaten the South's slave system?
_____
_____
_____

Free African Americans posed a threat to the institution of slavery. Many whites believed the African American could not survive outside of slavery. They used this as justification for slavery. The free African Americans could prove this theory wrong.

CHALLENGE ACTIVITY

Critical Thinking: Evaluate How effective were the laws limiting the rights of free African Americans? Write five questions that could be answered by historical study and outline research that could help you answer your questions.

DIRECTIONS Read each sentence and fill in the blank with the word
in the word pair that best completes the sentence.

1. The _____ were the wealthiest members of southern
society. (yeomen/planters).

2. Most white southerners were _____, or owners of small
farms, and owned few slaves or none at all. (yeomen/planters)

3. _____ would often work side by side with slaves.
(yeomen/planters)

4. In most southern cities, _____ did most of the work.
(planters/slaves)

5. White southerners shared a common culture and _____
that was central to southern social life. (artisans/religion)

6. Free African Americans in the South often worked as skilled

_____, or would hire out their services to plantations.

(artisans/religion)

7. Some wealthy white southerners attempted to use _____ to
justify their position in society and the institution of slavery. (artisans/religion)

DIRECTIONS On a separate sheet of paper use the vocabulary word
yeoman to write a letter that relates to the section.

The South

MAIN IDEAS
1. Slaves worked at a variety of jobs on plantations.
2. Life under slavery was difficult and dehumanizing.
3. Slave culture centered around family, community, and religion.
4. Slave uprisings led to stricter slave codes in many states.

Key Terms and People

folktales stories with a moral

spirituals songs that combine African and European music and religious beliefs

Nat Turner's Rebellion the name given to the 1831 rebellion led by Nat Turner

Nat Turner Virginia slave who led a rebellion against slaveholders in 1831

Academic Vocabulary

aspect part

Section Summary

SLAVES AND WORK

Most planters used the gang labor system to get their fields farmed. In this system enslaved men, women, and children over 10 years of age all did the same fieldwork from dawn until dark.

Slaves with special skills often were rented out by their owners. Sometimes these slaves were allowed to keep part of what they earned. As a consequence, some skilled slaves were able to save enough money to buy their own freedom.

How could skilled slaves buy their freedom?

_____
_____
_____

LIFE UNDER SLAVERY

To most southern slaveholders, slaves were property, not people. As property, slaves could be bought and sold. Usually, this business occurred at a slave auction. At these auctions family members could be sold away from each other forever.

What could happen to family members at a slave auction?

_____
_____

Many slaveholders used cruel punishments to make sure their slaves stayed obedient. In addition, many states passed strict slave codes. These laws limited what slaves could do. For example, in some states it was illegal to teach slaves to read and write.

> **How were laws used to control slaves?**
> _____
> _____
> _____

SLAVE CULTURE

For enslaved African Americans, the family was the most important **aspect** of their lives. Parents made sure their children knew the African part of their history, including African customs and traditions. Since they could not read and write, they passed this information verbally. Some of their stories were **folktales**—stories with morals—to teach children how to survive slavery.

> **How did slaves keep their culture alive?**
> _____
> _____
> _____

Religion was also an important part of the culture of enslaved African Americans. Christian slaves believed that, in God's eyes, they were equal to anyone else. They held onto the hope that someday they would be freed. Often, these beliefs were expressed in the **spirituals** they sang.

SLAVE UPRISINGS

Enslaved African Americans found a variety of ways to protest their treatment. Some even ran away. But getting all the way North to freedom was filled with dangers and hardships. Most runaways were caught and forced to return.

Sometimes, slaves protested with violence. They risked certain punishment. This was true of Virginia slave **Nat Turner**. During **Nat Turner's Rebellion** in 1831, slaves killed about 60 white people. In the end, though, more that 100 slaves were killed, and Turner was executed. As a result, many states strengthened their slave codes.

> **When did Nat Turner's Rebellion occur?**
> _____
> _____

CHALLENGE ACTIVITY

Critical Thinking: Analyze Write a paragraph explaining why southern slaveholders would want to keep slaves from learning to read and write.

| folktale | Nat Turner's Rebellion | slave codes |
| Nat Turner | spirituals | |

DIRECTIONS Answer each question by writing a sentence that contains at least one word from the word bank.

1. What was a story with a moral called?

_____

_____

2. What did some slaves use to express their religious beliefs?

_____

_____

3. Who led the most violent slave revolt in the United States?

_____

_____

_____

4. What event in 1831 led to the death of about 60 white people in Virginia?

_____

_____

_____

5. What was one way slaveholders attempted to keep slaves under control?

_____

_____

_____

New Movements in America

Section 1

MAIN IDEAS

1. Millions of immigrants, mostly German and Irish, arrived in the United States despite anti-immigrant movements.
2. Industrialization led to the growth of cities.
3. American cities experienced urban problems due to rapid growth.

Key Terms and People

nativists people who opposed immigration

Know-Nothing Party political organization founded by nativists in 1849

middle class a social and economic level between the wealthy and the poor

tenements dirty, unsafe housing structures in which the cities' poor were forced to live

Academic Vocabulary

implicit understood though not clearly put into words

Section Summary

MILLIONS OF IMMIGRANTS ARRIVE

Between 1840 and 1860, more than four million immigrants came to the United States. Many came from Ireland, fleeing starvation that came with a terrible potato famine there. The famine also meant that many Irish immigrants arrived poor. These immigrants often got jobs working long hours for little pay.

Unlike the Irish, immigrants from Germany often arrived with some money. Many came to America after a revolution in their homeland. Others came for the opportunities America offered. Many bought farmland in America's Midwest. Others settled and worked in cities.

To many native-born Americans, the new immigrants posed an **implicit** threat. Americans worried that immigrants would take away their jobs. Immigrants would do the same work but for less money. The Americans also mistrusted immigrants

> **Compare and contrast Irish and German immigration between 1840 and 1860.**
>
> _____
>
> _____
>
> _____

> **Why did nativists worry about the increasing numbers of immigrants?**
>
> _____
>
> _____

who were Catholic. In Europe, Protestants and
Catholics had a history of conflicts.

Americans who opposed immigration for these
reasons were known as **nativists**. Together, the
nativists formed a political group called the **Know-
Nothing Party**, which tried to limit immigration.
Nativist complaints lessened as immigrants settled
into life in the United States.

RAPID GROWTH OF CITIES

In the mid-1800s, the Industrial Revolution
encouraged rapid growth in America's cities. The
jobs the Industrial Revolution created also helped
build a **middle class**—a social and economic level
between the wealthy and the poor. These new urban
dwellers enjoyed the culture in America's cities.
Libraries, clubs, and theaters grew as the cities
grew.

> **Why do you think culture changed after the Industrial Revolution?**
> _____
> _____

URBAN PROBLEMS

The people who moved to the city to work could
afford only tenement rents. **Tenements** were poorly
designed housing structures that were dirty,
overcrowded, and unsafe. Cities had not yet learned
how to deal with the filth and garbage generated by
so many people, and killer epidemics resulted.
Crime and fires also plagued the fast-growing cities
of the United States.

> **Why were living conditions so poor in urban areas?**
> _____
> _____

CHALLENGE ACTIVITY

Critical Thinking: Summarize List some of the
health and safety issues that plagued America's
cities during the first half of the 1800s.

| immigrants | Know-Nothing Party | middle class |
| nativists | tenements | |

DIRECTIONS Read each sentence and choose the correct term from the word bank to replace the underlined phrase. Write the term in the space provided and then define the term in your own words.

1. A new social class, the <u>nativists</u>, occupied a social and economic level between the wealthy and the poor. _____

   Your definition: _____

   _____

2. Many city dwellers could only afford to live in poorly designed housing structures called <u>immigrants</u>. _____

   Your definition: _____

   _____

3. The nativists founded a political organization called the <u>middle class</u>. _____

   Your definition: _____

   _____

4. <u>Tenements</u> were Americans who held views such as fearing that new immigrants might work for lower wages and take away their jobs. _____

   Your definition: _____

   _____

5. In the mid-1800s, a flood of <u>nativists</u> crossed the Atlantic Ocean to begin new lives in the United States. _____

   Your definition: _____

   _____

> **MAIN IDEAS**
> 1. Transcendentalists and utopian communities withdrew from American society.
> 2. American Romantic painters and writers made important contributions to art and literature.

Key Terms and People

transcendentalism belief that people should rise above material things in life and that people should depend on themselves rather than outside authority

Ralph Waldo Emerson American writer most famous for his essay "Self-Reliance"

Margaret Fuller American writer who wrote and edited material on transcendentalism

Henry David Thoreau American writer most famous for the transcendental ideas he summarized in his book *Walden*

utopian communities experimental communities that tried to create a perfect society

Nathaniel Hawthorne American writer best known for his novel *The Scarlet Letter*

Edgar Allan Poe American writer best known for his short stories and poetry

Emily Dickinson American poet whose poems were published after her death

Henry Wadsworth Longfellow American poet who wrote popular story-poems like *The Song of Hiawatha*

Walt Whitman American poet best known for his poem *Leaves of Grass*

Academic Vocabulary

abstract expressing an idea without reference to an actual thing

Section Summary
TRANSCENDENTALISTS

Transcendentalism was a belief system in which followers thought they could rise above the material things in life. Transcendentalists believed that people should depend on themselves rather than outside authority. **Ralph Waldo Emerson, Margaret Fuller**, and **Henry David Thoreau** were

> Name two transcendentalist thinkers.
> _____
> _____

among the great American thinkers who were also transcendentalists.

Emerson expressed his ideas in the essay "Self-Reliance." Fuller wrote *Women in the Nineteenth Century*, a book about women's basic rights. In his book *Life in the Woods*, Thoreau summarized many of his transcendentalist beliefs.

Some transcendentalists created communities apart from society. In these **utopian communities**, people hoped to form a perfect society. Some, such as the Shaker communities, were based on religious beliefs. Other groups pursued utopian lifestyles for **abstract** and transcendental reasons.

> Why might transcendentalists seek to create utopian communities?
>
> _____
>
> _____

AMERICAN ROMANTICISM

In the early and mid-1800s, many artists were inspired by simple life and nature's beauty. Some joined the Romantic movement that began in Europe with British poets such as Blake, Byron, Keats, and Shelley. For the Romantics, each person brought a unique point of view to the world. These writers used their emotions to guide their words.

At this time Romantic writers developed an American style. American Romanticism let Americans see themselves as part of a European tradition of culture and as a new culture. **Nathaniel Hawthorne's** *Scarlet Letter* described Puritan life in America. Herman Melville wrote *Moby Dick*, one of America's finest novels. **Edgar Allan Poe** gained fame for his short stories and poetry.

Emily Dickinson, Henry Wadsworth Longfellow, and John Greenleaf Whittier are poets whose works have out-lived them. The same is true of **Walt Whitman**, whose poem *Leaves of Grass* praises American individualism and democracy.

> Underline all the writers' names that appear in this section. Put an 'X' by the names you have heard before.

> Circle the titles of famous novels written by American Romantics.

CHALLENGE ACTIVITY

Critical Thinking: Make Inferences In this section certain writers' names appear in bold print while other names do not. Explain what you think the difference is and why it is important.

DIRECTIONS Write two adjectives or descriptive phrases that describe the term.

1. Edgar Allan Poe _____

2. Emily Dickinson _____

3. Henry David Thoreau _____

4. Nathaniel Hawthorne _____

5. Ralph Waldo Emerson _____

6. Thomas Cole _____

7. transcendentalism _____

8. utopian communities _____

9. Walt Whitman _____

DIRECTIONS Read each sentence and fill in the blank with the word in the word pair that best completes the sentence.

10. "The Raven" is the most famous work by writer and poet

_____. (Ralph Waldo Emerson/Edgar Allan Poe)

11. _____ wrote *Leaves of Grass*.
(Nathaniel Hawthorne/Walt Whitman)

12. _____ edited the transcendentalist publication *The Dial*.
(Margaret Fuller/Emily Dickenson)

13. One of the best-known pieces of Romantic literature is *The Scarlet Letter*, a

novel by New England writer _____.

(Nathaniel Hawthorne/Walt Whitman)

14. _____ lived for two years at Walden Pond and wrote
about his beliefs in a book titled *Walden*. (Margaret Fuller/Henry David Thoreau)

New Movements in America

MAIN IDEAS

1. The Second Great Awakening sparked interest in religion.
2. Social reformers began to speak out about temperance and prison reform.
3. Improvements in education reform affected many parts of the population.
4. Northern African American communities became involved in reform efforts.

Key Terms and People

Second Great Awakening late 1700s-early 1800s movement of Christian renewal

Charles Grandison Finney minister who challenged some traditional beliefs

temperance movement movement to encourage people not to drink alcohol

Lyman Beecher minister who spoke against both Charles Grandison Finney and alcohol consumption

Dorothea Dix prison reformer

common-school movement movement to have all children, regardless of background, taught in a common place

Horace Mann education reformer

Catherine Beecher founder of all-female academy in Hartford, Connecticut

Thomas Gallaudet education reformer for the hearing impaired

Section Summary

SECOND GREAT AWAKENING

During the 1790s, a period of Christian renewal began. It was known as the **Second Great Awakening**. By the 1830s, it had swept through New England, the Appalachians, and the South.

    Charles Grandison Finney was one of the leaders of the Second Great Awakening. Some did not agree with Finney's message. However, the Constitution's First Amendment guaranteed Finney's right to speak and be heard. Through the efforts of Finney and other ministers, many Americans joined churches across the country.

> What can you infer from the fact that this period was called the Second Great Awakening?
>
> _____
>
> _____

SOCIAL REFORMERS SPEAK OUT

In the spirit of the Second Great Awakening, people tried to reform many of society's ills. In the **temperance movement**, people aimed at limiting alcohol consumption. **Lyman Beecher** and other ministers spoke about the evils of alcohol.

Another reformer, **Dorothea Dix**, reported on the terrible conditions she found when she visited some Massachusetts prisons. Imprisoned along with adult criminals were the mentally ill and children. Because of efforts by Dix and others, governments built hospitals for the mentally ill and reform schools for young lawbreakers. They also began to try to reform—not just punish—prisoners.

> How did prisons change as a result of reformers like Dorothea Dix?
>
> _____
>
> _____
>
> _____

IMPROVEMENTS IN EDUCATION

Education in the early 1800s improved with the **common-school movement**. This movement, led by **Horace Mann**, worked to have all students, regardless of background, taught in the same place. Women's education also improved at this time. Several women's schools, including **Catherine Beecher's** all-female academy in Connecticut, opened. Teaching people with disabilities improved, too. For example, **Thomas Gallaudet** bettered the education of the hearing impaired.

> What was the common-school movement?
>
> _____
>
> _____

AFRICAN AMERICAN COMMUNITIES

In this period, life improved for the nation's free black population. The Free Africans Religious Society, founded by Richard Allen, pressed for equality and education. Leaders such as Alexander Crummel helped build African American schools in New York, Philadelphia, and other cities. In 1835 Oberlin College became the first college to admit African Americans. Soon after, in the 1840s, several African American colleges were founded.

> Circle the names of all the reformers who worked to better America during this time.

CHALLENGE ACTIVITY

Critical Thinking: Compare and Contrast What did Horace Mann, Catherine Beecher, Thomas Gallaudet, and Richard Allen all have in common?

Guided Reading Workbook

Catharine Beecher	Lyman Beecher	common-school movement
Dorothea Dix	Charles Grandison Finney	Thomas Gallaudet
Horace Mann	Second Great Awakening	temperance movement

DIRECTIONS On the line provided before each statement, write **T** if a statement is true and **F** if a statement is false. If the statement is false, write the correct term on the line after each sentence that makes the sentence a true statement.

_____ 1. <u>Thomas Gallaudet</u> bettered the education and lives of people with hearing impairments.

_____

_____ 2. An all-female academy in Connecticut was started by <u>Dorothea Dix</u>.

_____

_____ 3. <u>Lyman Beecher</u> was a leader of the common-school movement.

_____

_____ 4. People in the <u>common-school movement</u> wanted all children taught in a common place, regardless of background.

_____

_____ 5. <u>Catharine Beecher</u> was a middle-class reformer who helped change the American prison system.

_____

_____ 6. Minister <u>Horace Mann</u> spoke widely about the evils of alcohol.

_____

_____ 7. A social reform effort that urged people to use self-discipline to stop drinking hard liquor was called the <u>temperance movement</u>.

_____

_____ 8. <u>Charles Grandison Finney</u> was one of the most important leaders of the Second Great Awakening.

_____

Section 4

> **MAIN IDEAS**
> 1. Americans from a variety of backgrounds actively opposed slavery.
> 2. Abolitionists organized the Underground Railroad to help enslaved Africans escape.
> 3. Despite efforts of abolitionists, many Americans remained opposed to ending slavery.

Key Terms and People

abolition complete end to slavery

William Lloyd Garrison abolitionist who ran the *Liberator* newspaper and also helped found the American Anti-Slavery Society

American Anti-Slavery Society organization that wanted immediate emancipation and racial equality

Angelina and Sarah Grimké southern sisters who spoke in favor of abolition

Frederick Douglass ex-slave who became a pro-abolition speaker

Sojourner Truth ex-slave who spoke for abolition and women's rights

Underground Railroad loosely organized group that helped slaves escape from the South

Harriet Tubman ex-slave who freed more than 300 others using the Underground Railroad

Section Summary
AMERICANS OPPOSE SLAVERY

By the 1830s, many Americans formed a movement to end slavery. They supported **abolition**. These abolitionists worked for emancipation, or freedom from slavery, for all who lived in the United States.

Some abolitionists thought that ex-slaves should get the same rights enjoyed by other Americans. Others, however, hoped to send the freed blacks back to Africa to start new colonies there. In fact, the American Colonization Society successfully founded the African colony of Liberia.

Many abolitionists spread the message of abolition using the power of the pen. **William Lloyd**

> What is the difference between abolition and emancipation?
>
> _____
> _____
> _____

Garrison, for example, ran the *Liberator* newspaper. He also helped found the **American Anti-Slavery Society**. This group believed in emancipation and racial equality. **Angelina and Sarah Grimké** were two sisters from a southern slave-holding family. They wrote pamphlets and a book to try to convince other white people to join the fight against slavery.

When **Frederick Douglass** was a slave, he secretly learned to read and write. After he escaped slavery, he used those skills to support the abolition movement by publishing a newspaper and writing books about his life. Douglass also was a powerful speaker who vividly described slavery's horrors. Many other ex-slaves also were active abolitionists. One example was **Sojourner Truth**, who became famous for her anti-slavery speeches.

> **Why do you think Frederick Douglass had to learn to read and write in secret?**
>
> _____
>
> _____
>
> _____

THE UNDERGROUND RAILROAD

The **Underground Railroad** was the name given a loosely knit group of white and black abolitionists who held escaped slaves get North to freedom. One of the most famous "conductors" on this Railroad was an ex-slave named **Harriet Tubman**. She made 19 trips to the north, freeing more than 300 slaves.

> **What do you think would happen to someone who was caught helping slaves escape?**
>
> _____
>
> _____

OPPOSITION TO ENDING SLAVERY

Many white southerners felt slavery was vital to their economy. They also felt that outsiders should not tell them what to do. Some justified enslaving people by claiming that African Americans needed the structure of slavery to survive.

CHALLENGE ACTIVITY

Critical Thinking: Make Inferences Why do you think Frederick Douglass called his newspaper the *North Star*?

DIRECTIONS Write two adjectives or descriptive phrases that describe the term.

1. abolition _____

2. American Anti-Slavery Society _____

3. American Colonization Society _____

4. Angelina and Sarah Grimké _____

5. Frederick Douglass _____

6. Harriet Tubman _____

7. the *Liberator* _____

8. Underground Railroad _____

9. William Lloyd Garrison _____

DIRECTIONS On the line provided before each statement, write **T** if a statement is true and **F** is a statement is false. If the statement is false, write the correct term on the line after each sentence that makes the sentence a true statement.

_____ 10. Some people who opposed slavery on religious grounds began working for the Underground Railroad.

_____

_____ 11. The American Anti-Slavery Society wanted to send freed African Americans to Africa to start new colonies.

_____

_____ 12. William Lloyd Garrison published an abolitionist newspaper called the *Liberator* and helped found the American Anti-Slavery Society.

_____

_____ 13. The most famous conductor on the Underground Railroad was Frederick Douglass.

_____

New Movements in America

 MAIN IDEAS

1. Influenced by the abolition movement, many women struggled to gain equal rights for themselves.
2. Calls for women's rights met opposition from men and women.
3. The Seneca Falls Convention launched the first organized women's rights movement in the United States.

Key Terms and People

Elizabeth Cady Stanton supporter of women's rights who helped organize the Seneca Falls Convention

Lucretia Mott women's rights supporter who helped organize the Seneca Falls Convention

Seneca Falls Convention the first organized public meeting about women's rights held in the United States

Declaration of Sentiments the document officially requesting equal rights for women

Lucy Stone spokesperson for the Anti-Slavery Society and the women's rights movement

Susan B. Anthony women's rights supporter who argued for equal pay for equal work, the right of women to enter traditionally male professions, and property rights

Section Summary

WOMEN'S STRUGGLE FOR EQUAL RIGHTS

In the mid-1800s, some female abolitionists also began to focus on the women's rights in America, despite their many critics. For example, the Grimké sisters were criticized for speaking in public. Their critics felt they should stay at home. Sarah Grimké responded by writing a pamphlet in support of women's rights. She also argued for equal educational opportunities, as well as for laws that treated women in an equal manner.

Abolitionist Sojourner Truth also became a women's-rights supporter. The ex-slave never learned to read or write, but she became a great and influential speaker.

> **Why did critics of the Grimké sisters think women should not speak in public?**
>
> _____
>
> _____

OPPOSING THE CALL FOR WOMEN'S RIGHTS

The women's movement had many critics—both men and women. Some felt a woman should stay home. Others felt women were not as physically or mentally strong as men. Therefore, they needed the protection of first their fathers, then their husbands. This was why upon marriage, husbands took control of their wives' property.

> **What arguments did critics use against women's rights?**
> _____
> _____

SENECA FALLS CONVENTION

With the support of leaders like **Elizabeth Cady Stanton** and **Lucretia Mott**, the **Seneca Falls Convention** opened July 19, 1848, in Seneca Falls, New York. It was the first time American women organized to promote women's rights. It resulted in the **Declaration of Sentiments**. This document officially requested equality for women. It brought 18 charges against men, much as the Declaration of Independence had brought 18 charges against King George III.

> **Why was the Seneca Falls Convention important?**
> _____
> _____

After the convention, more women rose to lead the fight for rights. **Lucy Stone**, for example, was another abolitionist who spoke out for women's rights. So did **Susan B. Anthony**. Anthony argued that women should be paid the same as men for the same job, and that women could do the jobs reserved for men. Anthony also fought for property rights for women. Many states changed their property laws because of her efforts. But some rights, such as the right to vote, were not won until much later.

> **Why do you think most of the leaders in the women's rights movement were women?**
> _____
> _____
> _____

CHALLENGE ACTIVITY

Critical Thinking: Evaluate Identify the women you think had the greatest impact on women's rights. Write a sentence or two explaining your choice.

DIRECTIONS Read each sentence and fill in the blank with the word
in the word pair that best completes the sentence.

1. _____ brought strong organizational skills to the women's
   rights movement. (Lucy Stone/Susan B. Anthony)

2. A well-known spokesperson for the Anti-Slavery Society who took up the cause

   of women's rights was _____. (Lucy Stone/Susan B. Anthony)

3. A powerful speaker for both abolition and women's rights was

   _____, who had been born into slavery.

   (Sojourner Truth/Lucy Stone)

4. _____ wanted to change the idea that women were not
   equal to men and helped organize a convention to discuss women's rights.
   (Sojourner Truth/Lucretia Mott)

5. _____ went to the World's Anti-Slavery Convention in
   England but was not allowed to participate because she was a woman. (Elizabeth
   Cady Stanton/Lucretia Mott)

6. The _____ was a public meeting organized by Elizabeth
   Cady Stanton and Lucretia Mott to discuss women's rights. (Seneca Falls
   Convention/Declaration of Sentiments)

7. Convention organizers wrote a document called the _____
   that detailed their beliefs about social injustice toward women. (Seneca Falls
   Convention/Declaration of Sentiments)

8. Several men, including _____, attended the Seneca Falls
   Convention. (T.S. Arthur/Frederick Douglass)

9. _____ never married, saying that the laws of the day gave
   husbands too much power over their wives. (Sojourner Truth/Sarah Grimké)

10. _____ collected more than 6,000 signatures on a petition
    that eventually led to the state of New York passing a law that allowed married
    women ownership of their wages and property. (Lucy Stone/Susan B. Anthony)

Guided Reading Workbook

	MAIN IDEAS **1.** The addition of new land in the West renewed disputes over the expansion of slavery. **2.** The Compromise of 1850 tried to solve the disputes over slavery. **3.** The Fugitive Slave Act caused more controversy. **4.** Abolitionists used antislavery literature to promote opposition.

Key Terms and People

popular sovereignty the idea that political power belongs to the people

Wilmot Proviso suggested bill that would outlaw slavery in new U.S. territory

sectionalism situation in which people favor the interests of one region over those of the entire country

Free-Soil Party third political party that formed to support abolition

Compromise of 1850 law that maintained America's slave-state/free-state balance

Fugitive Slave Act law that made it a crime to aid runaway slaves

Anthony Burns Virginia slave-fugitive whose attempted rescue from a Boston jail ended in violence

Uncle Tom's Cabin antislavery novel written by Harriet Beecher Stowe

Harriet Beecher Stowe author of the antislavery novel, *Uncle Tom's Cabin*

Section Summary
NEW LAND RENEWS SLAVERY DISPUTES

The nation's debate over slavery continued as the country got bigger. Many northerners for example, supported the **Wilmot Proviso**, which would outlaw slavery in new lands. Many southerners, on the other hand, did not support the bill. Arguments about the proviso showed how **sectionalism** was dividing the country.

Some favored the idea of **popular sovereignty**. They thought each region's voters should decide the question of slavery for that region. The debate was so intense that a third political party, the **Free-Soil Party**, formed to support abolition.

> **Why do you think southerners were opposed to the Wilmot Proviso?**
>
> _____
>
> _____
>
> _____

COMPROMISE OF 1850

The **Compromise of 1850** was presented by
Kentucky's Henry Clay. Its purpose was to maintain
the delicate balance between slave and free states. It
became law because of support by representatives
like Senator Daniel Webster.

What made Henry Clay's law a compromise?
_____
_____
_____

FUGITIVE SLAVE ACT

Part of the Compromise of 1850 required passage of
the **Fugitive Slave Act**. This act made it a crime to
help runaway slaves. Abolitionists especially
reacted in anger to the Compromise. Sometimes that
anger turned to violence. This was true when
abolitionists tried to rescue Virginia fugitive
Anthony Burns from a Boston jail.

How can you tell that Anthony Burns was a slave?
_____
_____
_____

ANTISLAVERY LITERATURE

Many abolitionists expressed their antislavery
feelings in speeches. Others used the written word
to influence people on the issue of slavery. One
effective author was **Harriet Beecher Stowe**. In
1852 Stowe's antislavery novel, *Uncle Tom's
Cabin*, was published. The book showed some of
the consequences of slavery. It sold more than
2 million copies and influenced many to support the
end of slavery.

How did Harriet Beecher Stowe impact the issue of slavery in America?
_____
_____
_____

CHALLENGE ACTIVITY

Critical Thinking: Write to Identify Write a
paragraph about something you read or saw that
made you change your mind. It could be a book, a
speech, a television show—even a teacher.

DIRECTIONS Read each sentence and fill in the blank with the word
in the word pair that best completes the sentence.

1. The _____ stated that "neither slavery nor involuntary
   servitude shall ever exist in any part of [the] territory."
   (Fugitive Slave Act/Wilmot Proviso)

2. When people favor the interests of one region over those of the entire country,

   this is called _____. (popular sovereignty/sectionalism)

3. _____ is where voters in a new territory decided if they
   wanted to ban or allow slavery. (popular sovereignty/sectionalism)

4. _____ was the author of an antislavery novel called

   _____. (Anthony Burns/Harriet Beecher Stowe);

   (Compromise of 1850/*Uncle Tom's Cabin*)

5. _____, a Virginia fugitive, was arrested in Boston and
   eventually returned to slavery in Virginia. (Anthony Burns/Daniel Webster)

6. Antislavery northerners formed a third party called the

   _____. (Free-Soil Party/Wilmot Proviso)

7. _____ came up with the plan called the

   _____, which allowed California to enter the Union as a

   free state while the question of slavery in Utah and New Mexico would be

   decided by popular sovereignty. (Anthony Burns/Henry Clay);

   (Compromise of 1850/Wilmot Proviso)

8. _____ of Massachusetts supported the Compromise of 1850
   and criticized northern abolitionists. (Daniel Webster/Harriet Beecher Stowe)

9. The _____ made it a crime to help runaway slaves.
   (Fugitive Slave Act/Wilmot Proviso)

A Divided Nation

MAIN IDEAS
1. The debate over the expansion of slavery influenced the election of 1852.
2. The Kansas-Nebraska Act allowed voters to allow or prohibit slavery.
3. Pro-slavery and antislavery groups clashed violently in what became known as "Bleeding Kansas."

Key Terms and People

Franklin Pierce Democratic candidate who won the presidential election of 1852

Stephen Douglas representative who introduced what would become the Kansas-Nebraska Act

Kansas-Nebraska Act the law that divided the rest of the Louisiana Purchase into two territories—Kansas and Nebraska

Pottawatomie Massacre the murder of five pro-slavery men at Pottawatomie Creek by John Brown and several other abolitionists

Charles Sumner Massachusetts senator who was an outspoken critic of pro-slavery leaders

Preston Brooks South Carolina representative who used a cane to beat Charles Sumner on the Senate floor for his criticisms of pro-slavery leaders

Academic Vocabulary

implications effects of a decision

Section Summary

ELECTION OF 1852

In the presidential election of 1852, the Democrats nominated **Franklin Pierce**. He was not a well-known politician, however his promise to honor the Compromise of 1850 assured him many southern votes. Pierce ran against Whig candidate Winfield Scott.

Pierce's win over Scott was resounding. When the votes were counted, it was discovered that out of the 31 states, 27 voted for Pierce.

> Why was Franklin Pierce a popular candidate in the South?
> _____
> _____

THE KANSAS-NEBRASKA ACT

The slavery issue continued to plague the United States. In 1854, Representative **Stephen Douglas** introduced a bill that addressed slavery in the Louisiana Territory. When it was signed into law on May 30, it became known as the **Kansas-Nebraska Act**. It got its name from the two territories into which it divided the rest of Louisiana—Kansas and Nebraska. In each territory, popular sovereignty would determine the answer to the slavery question.

To make sure Kansas voted in favor of slavery, pro-slavery voters left their homes in Missouri to cross the border and vote in Kansas. They won and quickly set up a pro-slavery government. However those who did not believe in slavery set up another, separate government in Topeka.

> **How did the Kansas-Nebraska Act get its name?**
> _____
> _____
> _____

> **What do you think would be the consequences of one state having two governments?**
> _____
> _____

"BLEEDING KANSAS"

In May 1856, pro-slavery jurors charged antislavery leaders with treason. Pro-slavery forces rode to Lawrence to arrest those charged. When they found the suspects had fled, they burned and looted the town.

The Sack of Lawrence outraged many abolitionists, including New England abolitionist John Brown. Together with a small group that included four of his sons, Brown was responsible for the **Pottawatomie Massacre**, in which five pro-slavery men were killed. Quickly, Kansas fell into civil war.

Fighting even took place on the Senate floor. South Carolina Representative **Preston Brooks** used his cane to beat Massachusetts Senator **Charles Sumner** into unconsciousness because of Sumner's criticisms of pro-slavery leaders.

> **What caused the Sack of Lawrence?**
> _____
> _____
> _____
> _____

> **Was Senator Charles Sumner for or against slavery?**
> _____
> _____
> _____

CHALLENGE ACTIVITY

Critical Thinking: Write to Explain Write a few sentences to explain how Kansas got the nickname "Bleeding Kansas."

Preston Brooks	John Brown	Stephen Douglas
Kansas-Nebraska Act	Franklin Pierce	Pottawatomie Massacre
Charles Sumner		

DIRECTIONS On the line provided before each statement, write **T** if a statement is true and **F** if a statement is false. If the statement is false, write the correct term on the line after each sentence that makes the sentence a true statement.

_____ 1. <u>Franklin Pierce</u> attacked Charles Sumner in the Senate chamber and beat him unconscious with a cane.

_____

_____ 2. Democratic candidate <u>Stephen Douglas</u> won the presidential election of 1852.

_____

_____ 3. <u>Preston Brooks</u>, a senator from Massachusetts, spoke out against the pro-slavery people in Kansas and was beaten by a fellow senator.

_____

_____ 4. The <u>Pottawatomie Massacre</u> resulted in the deaths of five pro-slavery men in Kansas.

_____

_____ 5. Senator <u>Stephen Douglas</u> introduced the Kansas-Nebraska Act.

_____

_____ 6. The <u>Kansas-Nebraska Act</u> divided part of the Louisiana Purchase into two territories—Kansas and Nebraska.

_____

_____ 7. Abolitionist <u>John Brown</u> and his sons moved to Kansas in 1855 and began to "strike terror in the hearts of the pro-slavery people."

_____ 8. The <u>Pottawatomie Massacre</u> removed the Missouri Compromise's restriction on slavery north of the 36°30′ line of latitude.

A Divided Nation

MAIN IDEAS
1. Political parties in the United States underwent change due to the movement to expand slavery.
2. The *Dred Scott* decision created further division over the issue of slavery.
3. The Lincoln-Douglas debates brought much attention to the conflict over slavery.

Key Terms and People

Republican Party political party founded to fight slavery

James Buchanan Democratic candidate and winner of the 1856 presidential election

John C. Frémont Republic candidate for the 1856 presidential election

Dred Scott slave who unsuccessfully sued for his freedom in 1846

Roger B. Taney Chief Justice of the Supreme Court during the *Dred Scott* decision

Abraham Lincoln early leader of the Republican Party

Lincoln-Douglas debates debates between senatorial candidates Abraham Lincoln and Stephen Douglas

Freeport Doctrine Stephen Douglas's belief in popular sovereignty, stated during the Freeport debate

Academic Vocabulary

complex difficult; not simple

Section Summary
POLITICAL PARTIES UNDERGO CHANGE

As the 1850s progressed Whigs, Democrats, Free-Soilers, and abolitionists united to create the **Republican Party** to fight slavery. Others left their parties to form the Know-Nothing Party. For the 1856 presidential election, the old Democratic Party nominated **James Buchanan**. Buchanan had been out of the country during the Kansas bloodshed, but he defeated Know-Nothing Millard Fillmore and Republican **John C. Frémont**.

> **Why might it matter to voters that James Buchanan had been out of the country during "Bleeding Kansas"?**
>
> _____
> _____
> _____

DRED SCOTT DECISION

Dred Scott was a slave. His slaveowner was a doctor who traveled from Missouri, a slave state, to free areas and back again to Missouri. Scott sued for his freedom, since he had lived in free states.

The Supreme Court's decision in this **complex** case was against Scott. Chief Justice **Roger B. Taney** wrote that African Americans were not citizens, and only citizens could sue in federal court. Taney also wrote in the Dred Scott decision that slaves were considered property, and Scott living in free territory did not make him free. Taney said that Congress could not stop people from taking slaves into federal territory.

Many antislavery voices rose against the decision. This included the voice of an Illinois lawyer named **Abraham Lincoln**.

LINCOLN-DOUGLAS DEBATES

In 1858 Abraham Lincoln ran for a U.S. Senate seat as the Republican candidate. His opponent was Democrat Stephen Douglas, who was up for reelection. During the campaign, the two men met several times in what became known as the **Lincoln-Douglas debates**. In the debates, Lincoln was careful not to talk about slavery in the existing slave states. Instead, he claimed the Democrats were trying to spread slavery across the nation.

During the second debate, Lincoln questioned Douglas about popular sovereignty. He wondered whether that belief went against the *Dred Scott* decision. In other words, how could the people ban what the Supreme Court allowed? Douglas restated his belief in popular sovereignty. His response was remembered as the **Freeport Doctrine**.

CHALLENGE ACTIVITY

Critical Thinking: Write to Summarize Write a paragraph summarizing the impact of the Fifth Amendment on the Supreme Court's ruling in the *Dred Scott* case.

> Underline the three decisions the Supreme Court made in the *Dred Scott* case.

> Are you surprised to know that at the time of the *Dred Scott* decision, a majority of Supreme Court Justices were from the South? Why or why not?

> Why do you believe Lincoln would not talk about slavery in the existing slave states?

> Why did Lincoln question the Democrats' belief in popular sovereignty?

DIRECTIONS Write two adjectives or descriptive phrases that describe the term.

1. Abraham Lincoln _____

_____

2. Dred Scott _____

_____

3. *Dred Scott* decision _____

_____

4. Freeport Doctrine _____

_____

5. James Buchanan _____

_____

6. John C. Frémont _____

_____

7. Lincoln-Douglas debates _____

_____

8. Republican Party _____

_____

9. Roger B. Taney _____

_____

10. Stephen Douglas _____

_____

A Divided Nation

MAIN IDEAS
1. John Brown's raid on Harpers Ferry intensified the disagreement between free states and slave states.
2. The outcome of the election of 1860 divided the United States.
3. The dispute over slavery led the South to secede.

Key Terms and People

John Brown's raid Brown's attack on the Harpers Ferry arsenal, which began October 16, 1859

John C. Breckinridge pro-slavery candidate nominated by southern Democrats for the 1860 presidential election

Constitutional Union Party new political party that concentrated on constitutional principles

John Bell candidate nominated for the 1860 election by the Constitutional Union Party

Confederate States of America the country formed by seceding southern states

Jefferson Davis the Confederacy's first president

John J. Crittenden Tennessee senator who proposed a compromise to try to stop southern secession

Section Summary
RAID ON HARPERS FERRY

John Brown was an abolitionist. He decided to use violence to try to stop slavery. He planned to lead an attack on the arsenal at Harpers Ferry, Virginia.

John Brown's raid began on October 16, 1859. Although he succeeded in taking the arsenal, federal troops overwhelmed him and his small band. They killed some of Brown's followers and captured others, including Brown himself. Brown was charged and found guilty. On December 2, 1859, he was hanged for his crimes.

> When did John Brown's raid begin?
>
> _____
>
> _____

Many northerners agreed with Brown's anti-slavery beliefs, but they did not agree with his violent methods. Southerners worried that Brown's raid was the start of more attacks on the South.

> **Why do you think John Brown's raid scared southerners?**
> _____
> _____

ELECTION OF 1860

The country was torn as the 1860 presidential election approached. The Democrats proposed two candidates—the North's Stephen Douglas and the South's **John C. Breckinridge**. In addition, the new **Constitutional Union Party** nominated **John Bell** to run on a platform against the idea of states' rights. Abraham Lincoln ran on the Republican ticket.

Lincoln won the election, but he did not carry a southern state in his win. This angered southerners, who worried that they had lost their political power.

> **Underline the names of the presidential candidates who ran for election in 1860.**

THE SOUTH SECEDES

Southern states responded to Lincoln's election with secession. These states joined together into a new country—the **Confederate States of America**. They elected Mississippian **Jefferson Davis** as their first president. In this country, slavery was legal.

Lincoln argued that southern states could not secede. It seemed that even compromises, like one proposed by Kentucky Senator **John J. Crittenden**, would not mend this tear in the national fabric. President-elect Lincoln declared there could be no compromise where slavery was concerned. He also announced that the federal property in southern lands remained part of the United States.

> **What event led southern states to secede from the United States of America?**
> _____
> _____
> _____
> _____

CHALLENGE ACTIVITY

Critical Thinking: Write to Analyze Write a paragraph explaining why the Democrats ran two candidates in the 1860 presidential election and the affect that had on the South's secession.

DIRECTIONS Write a word or phrase that means the opposite of the term given.

1. Confederate States of America _____

_____

2. secession _____

_____

DIRECTIONS Read each sentence and fill in the blank with the word in the word pair that best completes the sentence.

3. _____ was an attack on the arsenal at Harpers Ferry, Virginia in 1859. (secession/John Brown's raid)

4. During the election of 1860, a new political party emerged called the

_____.

(Constitutional Union Party/Confederate States of America)

5. _____ was chosen as the Constitutional Union Party's candidate for president. (John J. Crittenden/John Bell)

6. _____ was elected president of the

_____. (John J. Crittenden/Jefferson Davis);

(Constitutional Union Party/Confederate States of America)

7. Senator _____ from Kentucky proposed a series of constitutional amendments he hoped would satisfy the South and save the Union. (John J. Crittenden/John Bell)

8. Abolitionist John Brown was executed for his part in the raid on

_____. (Harpers Ferry/Confederate States of America)

The Civil War

> **MAIN IDEAS**
> **1.** Following the outbreak of war at Fort Sumter, Americans chose sides.
> **2.** The Union and the Confederacy prepared for war.

Key Terms and People

Fort Sumter federal post in Charleston, South Carolina, that surrendered to the Confederacy

border states four slave states—Delaware, Kentucky, Maryland, and Missouri—that bordered the North

Winfield Scott Union general with a two-part strategy for defeating the Confederacy

cotton diplomacy Confederate plan to enlist England's aid in return for continued cotton shipments

Section Summary
AMERICANS CHOOSE SIDES

After being elected in 1860, Abraham Lincoln took office as seven southern states left the Union. He promised he would not end slavery where it existed. However, he also promised to preserve the Union.

Confederate officials already were taking control of federal mints, arsenals, and forts. Fighting finally broke out at **Fort Sumter**, a federal fort in the Confederate state of South Carolina. Federal troops refused to surrender to the Confederacy. Within two days, Fort Sumter fell. Lincoln called for 75,000 militiamen to put down the South's rebellion.

After Lincoln called for troops, all the states had to choose a side. Four more slave states joined the Confederacy. Four **border states**—slave states that bordered the North—decided to stay in the Union. In addition, western Virginia broke off from Confederate Virginia to stay in the Union.

Union General **Winfield Scott** had a two-part strategy to conquer the South. First he would destroy its economy with a naval blockade. Second

> How did the South react to Lincoln's election to the presidency?
>
> _____
>
> _____

> How did Lincoln respond to the surrender of Fort Sumter?
>
> _____
>
> _____

he would gain control of the Mississippi River to help divide the South.

The Confederacy had its own plan of attack. Part of that plan involved **cotton diplomacy**—the hope that Britain would support the Confederacy because it needed Confederate cotton. This strategy did not work because Britain had large stores of cotton and got more from India and Egypt.

> **Why didn't cotton diplomacy work?**
> _____
> _____
> _____

PREPARING FOR WAR

Neither side was prepared for the war to come. However, many citizens—northern and southern—were eager to help. Thousands upon thousands of young men answered the call to arms and volunteered to serve in both armies.

Civilians, too, volunteered to help. They raised money to aid soldiers and their families. They staffed and supplied emergency hospitals. In the Union alone, about 3,000 women served as army nurses.

> **In what ways did civilians help the war effort?**
> _____
> _____
> _____

Once the thousands of farmers, teachers, laborers, and others joined the armies, they had to be trained to become soldiers. They spent long days drilling and practicing with their guns and bayonets. As a result, many young soldiers were ready to fight.

CHALLENGE ACTIVITY

Critical Thinking: Write to Influence Write an advertisement encouraging people to support the soldiers by coming to a fundraising event.

| border states | cotton diplomacy | Fort Sumter |
| Abraham Lincoln | Winfield Scott | |

DIRECTIONS Use the five vocabulary words from the word list to
write a summary of what you learned in the section.

_____

_____

_____

_____

_____

_____

_____

_____

DIRECTIONS Read each sentence and fill in the blank with the word
in the word pair that best completes the sentence.

1. The Civil War began in 1861 when Confederate troops began to fire on
   _____ (border states/Fort Sumter)

2. Union General _____ planned to destroy the South's economy
   with a naval blockade of southern ports. (Abraham Lincoln/Winfield Scott)

3. The South tried to win foreign allies through _____.
   (border states/cotton diplomacy)

4. In his inaugural address, _____ promised not to end
   slavery where it existed. (Abraham Lincoln/Winfield Scott)

5. Delaware, Kentucky, Maryland, and Missouri were _____
   that did not join the Confederacy. (border states/cotton diplomacy)

The Civil War

MAIN IDEAS

1. Union and Confederate forces fought for control of the war in Virginia.
2. The Battle of Antietam gave the North a slight advantage.
3. The Confederacy attempted to break the Union naval blockade.

Key Terms and People

Thomas "Stonewall" Jackson Confederate general who helped fight Union troops at the First Battle of Bull Run

First Battle of Bull Run battle near Manassas Junction, Virginia, in 1861

George B. McClellan general sent by President Lincoln to capture Richmond

Robert E. Lee Confederate general during many important battles of the Civil War

Seven Days' Battles series of battles that forced McClellan to retreat from near Richmond

Second Battle of Bull Run Confederate attack that helped push Union forces out of Virginia

Battle of Antietam battle in Maryland that resulted in Lee's retreat to Virginia

ironclads ships that were heavily armored with iron

Academic Vocabulary

innovation a new idea or way of doing something

Section Summary
WAR IN VIRGINIA

In July 1861, the Union and Confederate armies clashed near Manassas Junction, Virginia, along Bull Run Creek. At first the Union soldiers, under General Irvin McDowell, pushed back the left side of the Confederate line. Then Southern troops, inspired by General **Thomas "Stonewall" Jackson**, fought back. With reinforcements arriving, the Confederate troops drove the Union army back. This conflict, called the **First Battle of Bull Run**, showed that the war would not be an easy victory for the Union.

> **What did the First Battle of Bull Run show?**
> _____
> _____
> _____

After the failed attempt to take Richmond, Lincoln tried again. This time he sent new commander General **George B. McClellan**. In the spring of 1862, McClellan led 100,000 soldiers on a slow march to Richmond.

Then, in June, General **Robert E. Lee** took command of the Confederate forces. On June 26 the two armies met in the **Seven Days' Battles**. These battles pushed McClellan away from Richmond. During the **Second Battle of Bull Run**, Jackson's troops defeated another Union army before it could march directly on Richmond.

> Underline all the Civil War battles identified on this page.

BATTLE OF ANTIETAM

A copy of Lee's battle strategy left behind led to the next major battle of the Civil War. The Union discovered the Confederates were going to attack Harpers Ferry. McClellan sent his troops to stop them. The **Battle of Antietam** took place on September 17, 1862. It halted Lee's northward march. Despite this success the battle was the bloodiest of the Civil War and of United States history.

BREAKING THE UNION'S BLOCKADE

Despite the distance it had to control, the Union blockade of Southern ports was very effective. It reduced the number of ships entering southern ports from 6,000 to 800 per year. Even though both sides had the **innovation** of **ironclads**, the Union continued the blockade unbroken.

> Circle the sentence that supports the statement that the Union blockade of Southern ports was very effective.

CHALLENGE ACTIVITY

Critical Thinking: Explain How was a mistake responsible for the Battle of Antietam?

Battle of Antietam	Seven Days' Battles	ironclads
Robert E. Lee	George B. McClellan	First Battle of Bull Run
Second Battle of Bull Run	Thomas "Stonewall" Jackson	

DIRECTIONS Use five of the vocabulary words from the word list to write a letter that relates to the section.

Dear _____ ,

_____

_____

_____

_____

DIRECTIONS On the line provided before each statement, write **T** if a statement is true and **F** if a statement is false. If the statement is false, write the correct term on the line after each sentence that makes the sentence a true statement.

_____ 1. Abraham Lincoln had asked <u>George B. McClellan</u> to lead the Union army, but he declined and resigned his commission to become a general in the Confederate army.

_____

_____ 2. The <u>Battle of Antietam</u> was the bloodiest single-day battle of the Civil War, with a total of more than 25,000 casualties.

_____

_____ 3. The North's hopes of winning the war quickly and easily were crushed when the Union army was defeated at the <u>Second Battle of Bull Run</u>.

_____

_____ 4. General <u>Thomas "Stonewall" Jackson</u> led Confederate troops to victory during the First Battle of Bull Run.

_____

MAIN IDEAS
1. Union strategy in the West centered on control of the Mississippi River.
2. Confederate and Union troops struggled for dominance in the Far West.

Key Terms and People

Ulysses S. Grant Union general whose troops won several important battles on southern soil

Battle of Shiloh battle in which Union troops gained greater control of the Mississippi River valley

David Farragut naval leader who helped the Union take control of New Orleans

Siege of Vicksburg six-week blockade of Vicksburg that starved the city into surrender

Section Summary
UNION STRATEGY IN THE WEST

In February 1862 General **Ulysses S. Grant** led a Union army into Tennessee. He was headed toward the Mississippi River to capture outposts that would separate the eastern Confederacy from its western, food-supplying states. On the way Grant and his forces took both Fort Henry and Fort Donelson.

Near Shiloh Church, Grant halted his troops to wait for more soldiers to arrive. Although Grant was aware of Confederate troops in the area, he was caught by surprise when they attacked on April 6. During the two-day **Battle of Shiloh**, each side lost and gained ground. Union reinforcements arrived and helped push the Confederates into retreating. This win helped the Union control part of the Mississippi River valley.

To control the Mississippi River, the Union had to first deal with New Orleans, the south's largest city and the valuable port near the mouth of the Mississippi River. However, two forts guarded New Orleans from the south.

> Why did the Union consider control of the Mississippi River critical?
>
> _____
> _____
> _____

> How do you know that Fort Henry and Fort Donelson were Confederate forts?
>
> _____
> _____
> _____

> How was New Orleans captured?
>
> _____
> _____
> _____

Union Admiral **David Farragut** solved that problem by racing past the two forts in the darkness before dawn on April 24, 1862. Within days New Orleans fell to the Union troops. Farragut continued north, taking more cities, until he reached Vicksburg, Mississippi.

Vicksburg was located on cliffs high above the Mississippi River which allowed Confederate General John C. Pemberton to stop any attempt to attack the city. So, instead of trying to attack Vicksburg directly, General Grant cut the city off and shelled it repeatedly. The **Siege of Vicksburg** lasted about six weeks before hunger forced the Confederates to surrender. The Mississippi River was now under Union control.

Why was Vicksburg difficult to capture?
_____
_____
_____

STRUGGLE FOR THE FAR WEST

Fighting also broke out in the southwest, as the Confederates tried to take control there. Defeats in Arizona and at Glorieta Pass stopped Confederates from taking lands in the West. Confederate-Union conflicts in Missouri also ended with a Confederate defeat, despite aid from the Cherokee. Attacks on Union forts and raids on towns forced the Union commanders to keep valuable troops stationed in the western states and territories.

Why did the siege of Vicksburg succeed when attacks on Vicksburg had failed?
_____
_____

CHALLENGE ACTIVITY

Critical Thinking: Analyze Write a paragraph analyzing why the Union wanted to control the West.

Battle of Shiloh	David Farragut	Ulysses S. Grant
John C. Pemberton	Siege of Vicksburg	

DIRECTIONS Answer each question by writing a sentence that contains at least one word from the word bank.

1. Which Union commander was the most important figure in the war in the West?

_____

_____

_____

2. Who was the Union naval leader from Tennessee who captured New Orleans?

_____

_____

_____

3. What is the name of the event where the Union army, under General Ulysses S. Grant, gained greater control of the Mississippi River?

_____

_____

_____

4. Who was the Confederate general who attempted to defend the city of Vicksburg, Mississippi, from Union attack?

_____

_____

_____

5. What event lasted about six weeks and ended when the Union captured Vicksburg, Mississippi?

_____

_____

_____

The Civil War

Section 4

> **MAIN IDEAS**
> 1. The Emancipation Proclamation freed slaves in Confederate states.
> 2. African Americans participated in the war in a variety of ways.
> 3. President Lincoln faced opposition to the war.
> 4. Life was difficult for soldiers and civilians alike.

Key Terms and People

emancipation the freeing of slaves

Emancipation Proclamation announcement freeing Confederate slaves

contrabands escaped slaves

54th Massachusetts Infantry heroic unit of African American soldiers

Copperheads nickname for the Peace Democrats

habeas corpus constitutional protection against unlawful imprisonment

Clara Barton army volunteer whose work became the basis for the American Red Cross

Section Summary

EMANCIPATION PROCLAMATION

President Lincoln realized that one way to weaken the South was to free the slaves. **Emancipation** would free many slaves on which the South's economy relied. After the Battle of Antietam, Lincoln presented the **Emancipation Proclamation**. Despite the impossibility of enforcing it in Confederate-held states, the proclamation still had a distinct effect on the war.

> What was the purpose of the Emancipation Proclamation?
>
> _____
>
> _____
>
> _____

AFRICAN AMERICANS PARTICIPATE IN THE WAR

In July 1862 Congress decided to allow African Americans to join the army as laborers. This decision included both free African Americans and **contrabands**, or escaped slaves. Within a year several African American units had formed, the most famous being the **54th Massachusetts Infantry**. These troops helped attack South Carolina's Fort Wagner.

> How were contrabands different from other African Americans who joined the Union army?
>
> _____
>
> _____

Guided Reading Workbook

African American soldiers received less pay than white soldiers. They also faced greater danger because, if captured by Confederates, they could be returned to slavery. In fact Lincoln suggested these soldiers be rewarded by getting the right to vote.

GROWING OPPOSITION

Some mid-westerners did not think the war was necessary. They called themselves Peace Democrats, but their enemies called them **Copperheads**, after the poisonous snake.

Because he saw them as a threat to the war effort, Lincoln had Copperheads put in jail with no evidence and no trial. To do this he ignored their right of **habeas corpus**, the constitutional protection against unlawful imprisonment. Despite this and the northern draft, Lincoln won his second election in 1864.

> **What is habeas corpus?**
> _____
> _____

LIFE FOR SOLDIERS AND CIVILIANS

For the soldier both camplife and combat offered dangers. Poor camp conditions, including lack of medicine and painkillers, led to illness. This alone killed more men than battle did. Those wounded or captured in battle often met the same fate.

Those left behind took over the work of the men who went to war. In addition, many women also provided medical care for the soldiers. For example, volunteer **Clara Barton** formed the organization that would become the American Red Cross.

> **How did women help the war effort?**
> _____
> _____

CHALLENGE ACTIVITY

Critical Thinking: Contrast First, imagine you are a lawyer for the Peace Democrats. Write a paragraph explaining why their right of habeas corpus should not be ignored. Then imagine you are a lawyer for the federal government. Write a paragraph defending Lincoln's actions.

DIRECTIONS Read each sentence and fill in the blank with the word
in the word pair that best completes the sentence.

1. The _____ called for all Confederate slaves to be freed.
   (habeas corpus/Emancipation Proclamation)

2. The _____ consisted mostly of free African Americans.
   (Emancipation Proclamation/54th Massachusetts Infantry)

3. _____ were a group of Northern Democrats who spoke out
   against the Civil War. (contrabands/Copperheads)

4. _____ is the constitutional protection against unlawful
   imprisonment. (habeas corpus/emancipation)

5. _____, who worked as a volunteer during the Civil War,
   organized the collection of medicine and supplies for delivery to Union troops on
   the battlefield. (Clara Barton/Copperheads)

6. The War Department gave _____, or escaped slaves, the
   right to join the Union army. (contrabands/Copperheads)

7. _____ is the freeing of slaves.
   (habeas corpus/emancipation)

8. President Lincoln suspended the right of _____ so that
   Union officials could put their enemies in jail without a trial.
   (habeas corpus/emancipation)

9. _____ helped found the American branch of the Red Cross.

   (Clara Barton/Copperheads)

10. Abraham Lincoln feared that the _____ would erode

    support for the war, so he ignored the right of _____ to silence

    them. (contrabands/Copperheads); (habeas corpus/emancipation)

The Civil War

MAIN IDEAS

1. The Union tried to divide the Confederate Army at Fredericksburg, but the attempt failed.
2. The Battle of Gettysburg in 1863 was a major turning point in the war.
3. During 1864 Union campaigns in the East and South dealt crippling blows to the Confederacy.
4. Union troops forced the South to surrender in 1865, ending the Civil War.

Key Terms and People

Battle of Gettysburg three-day battle that Confederates lost

George Pickett general who carried out Lee's orders to charge the Union line

Pickett's Charge disastrous attempt by Pickett's troops to storm Cemetery Ridge

Gettysburg Address speech in which Lincoln renewed his commitment to winning the war

Wilderness Campaign series of battles in which Grant tried to take Richmond

William Tecumseh Sherman Union general who cut a path of destruction across Georgia

Total War strategy in which both civilian and military resources are destroyed

Appomattox Courthouse the place where Lee surrendered to Grant

Academic Vocabulary

execute to perform, carry out

Section Summary

FREDERICKSBURG AND CHANCELLORSVILLE

In late 1862 Confederate troops under the command of General Robert E. Lee won a battle at Fredericksburg, Virginia. In the spring of 1863, they again defeated Union troops at Chancellorsville.

BATTLE OF GETTYSBURG

Hoping a Confederate win on Union soil would break the Union's spirit, Lee headed into Union territory. The **Battle of Gettysburg**, which started July 1, 1863, was the consequence.

> How did the Battle of Gettysburg start?
>
> _____
>
> _____

The first day, Lee's troops pushed General Meade's soldiers back. The Union troops had to dig in on top of two hills outside the town. On the second day, Confederate troops tried to take the hill called Little Round Top but failed.

On the third day, Lee ordered General **George Pickett** to lead a charge on Cemetery Ridge. **Pickett's Charge** was a disaster. Over half the Confederates were killed, and Lee retreated. Never again would his troops reach northern land.

President Lincoln helped dedicate a new cemetery at Gettysburg. On November 19, 1863, he delivered the **Gettysburg Address**.

> **How long did the Battle of Gettysburg last?**
> _____
> _____

> **Who won the Battle of Gettysburg?**
> _____
> _____

UNION CAMPAIGNS CRIPPLE THE CONFEDERACY

The **Wilderness Campaign** was a series of battles fought in Virginia, around Richmond. Although he lost more men than Lee, Grant also had more reinforcements. As a result of the battles, Grant was winning the war. However, at Petersburg, Lee's defenses did not allow Grant to **execute** his attack and capture Richmond.

To assure his re-election, Lincoln needed a victory. General **William Tecumseh Sherman** provided it by capturing Atlanta, Georgia. This victory helped Lincoln get re-elected in a landslide.

Sherman did not stop at Atlanta. He ordered his troops to cut a path of destruction through Georgia, practicing **total war** all the way to the ocean.

> **How did General William Sherman help President Lincoln get re-elected?**
> _____
> _____

THE SOUTH SURRENDERS

On April 9, 1865, at **Appomattox Courthouse**, Lee officially surrendered to Grant. The long, bloody war was over, but the question of how the United States could be united again remained.

> **In what year did the Civil War end?**
> _____
> _____

CHALLENGE ACTIVITY

Critical Thinking: Make a Time Line Use dates and events in this section to make a time line of the Civil War.

Appomattox Courthouse	Battle of Gettysburg	George Pickett
George G. Meade	Gettysburg Address	Pickett's Charge
total war	Wilderness Campaign	William Tecumseh Sherman

DIRECTIONS On the line provided before each statement, write **T** if a statement is true and **F** if a statement is false. If the statement is false, write the correct term on the line after each sentence that makes the sentence a true statement.

_____ 1. The <u>Battle of Gettysburg</u> was a turning point in the Civil War and made northerners believe the war could be won.

_____

_____ 2. The Battle of Gettysburg began when Confederate soldiers raided the city of Gettysburg and clashed with Union cavalry led by General <u>George G. Meade</u>.

_____

_____ 3. <u>William Tecumseh Sherman</u> commanded the largest unit of Confederate soldiers during the Battle of Gettysburg.

_____

_____ 4. Nearly 15,000 men took part in <u>total war</u>, which was a disastrous attack on Union forces at Cemetery Ridge during the Battle of Gettysburg.

_____

_____ 5. The <u>Wilderness Campaign</u>, given at the dedication of the cemetery at the Gettysburg battlefield, was a short but moving speech, and is one of the most famous speeches in American history.

_____

_____ 6. <u>William Tecumseh Sherman</u> carried out a campaign, known as total war, to destroy southern railroads and industries to ruin the South's economy and its ability to fight.

_____

Guided Reading Workbook

Reconstruction

 MAIN IDEAS
1. President Lincoln and Congress differed in their views as Reconstruction began.
2. The end of the Civil War meant freedom for African Americans in the South.
3. President Johnson's plan began the process of Reconstruction.

Key Terms and People

Reconstruction a period of reuniting and rebuilding the South following the end of the Civil War

Ten Percent Plan Lincoln's Reconstruction plan, which required that 10 percent of voters in a state pledge loyalty to the United States before that state could rejoin the Union

Thirteenth Amendment the amendment that made slavery illegal throughout the United States

Freedmen's Bureau an organization established by Congress to provide relief for all the South's poor people

Andrew Johnson vice president who became president upon Lincoln's death

Academic Vocabulary

procedure a series of steps taken to accomplish a task

Section Summary
RECONSTRUCTION BEGINS

As soon as the Civil War ended, Reconstruction began. **Reconstruction** was the process of reuniting the nation and rebuilding the southern states.

President Lincoln proposed that southerners be offered amnesty, or an official pardon. Southerners had to swear an oath of loyalty to the United States and accept the ban on slavery. When 10 percent of the voters in any state took the oath, that state could be accepted back into the Union. This was called the **Ten Percent Plan**.

Some supported the Wade-Davis Bill instead. The **procedure** of the Wade-Davis Bill asked southerners to ban slavery. However, under this bill,

> **What was the purpose of Reconstruction?**
> _____
> _____
> _____
> _____

most of the people of a state would have to take the
pledge before the state could rejoin the Union. Also,
only southerners who swore they had never
supported the Confederacy could run for office.
Lincoln vetoed it.

FREEDOM FOR AFRICAN AMERICANS

In 1865 the **Thirteenth Amendment** to the
Constitution officially outlawed slavery in the
nation. Former slaves reacted to freedom in many
ways. They legalized their marriages, searched for
relatives who had been sold, took last names, and
moved to new places.

> **What part of the Constitution granted freedom to all slaves?**
> _____
> _____

To help the South's poor and freedpeople
Congress created the **Freedmen's Bureau** in 1865.
One of its roles was to build more schools. Some
freedpeople also established their own schools.
Although some southerners violently resisted the
idea of educating African Americans, freedpeople
of all ages attended classes.

> **Why would southerners oppose the education of African Americans?**
> _____
> _____
> _____
> _____

PRESIDENT JOHNSON'S RECONSTRUCTION PLAN

On April 14, 1865, President Lincoln was shot
while attending the theater. He died the next
morning. Vice President **Andrew Johnson** became
the next president. Johnson's Reconstruction plan
included a way to restructure southern state
governments. States that followed the steps were to
be readmitted to the Union.

> **Why did Congress refuse to accept the southern states back into the Union?**
> _____
> _____
> _____
> _____

Most of the southern states followed Johnson's
plan, but Congress refused to accept them back into
the Union. Many of the elected representatives of
the "new" states had been Confederate leaders.
Clearly there were still problems to be solved.

CHALLENGE ACTIVITY

Critical Thinking: Write to Defend You are a
citizen from a southern state. Write a letter to
Congress defending your right to choose your
state's representatives.

| Andrew Johnson | Freedmen's Bureau | Reconstruction |
| Ten Percent Plan | Thirteenth Amendment | |

DIRECTIONS Read each sentence and choose the correct term from the word bank to replace the underlined phrase. Write the term in the space provided and then define the term in your own words.

1. The process of reuniting the nation and rebuilding the southern states without slavery was called <u>Ten Percent Plan</u>. _____

   Your definition: _____

2. The <u>Thirteenth Amendment</u> was established to provide relief for all poor people, black and white, in the South. _____

   Your definition: _____

3. <u>The Freedmen's Bureau</u> was the vice president sworn into office after President Lincoln was shot at Ford's Theater and later died. _____

   Your definition: _____

4. Lincoln offered southerners amnesty for all illegal acts supporting the rebellion under the <u>Thirteenth Amendment</u>. _____

   Your definition: _____

5. Slavery was made illegal throughout the United States under the <u>Ten Percent Plan</u>. _____

   Your definition: _____

Reconstruction

MAIN IDEAS
1. Black Codes led to opposition to President Johnson's plan for Reconstruction.
2. The Fourteenth Amendment ensured citizenship for African Americans.
3. Radical Republicans in Congress took charge of Reconstruction.
4. The Fifteenth Amendment gave African Americans the right to vote.

Key Terms and People

Black Codes southern laws that greatly limited the freedom of African Americans

Radical Republicans Republicans who wanted more federal control in Reconstruction

Civil Rights Act of 1866 act giving African Americans the same legal rights as whites

Fourteenth Amendment amendment guaranteeing citizens equal protection of laws

Reconstruction Acts laws passed to protect African American rights

impeachment process of bringing charges of wrongdoing against a public official

Fifteenth Amendment amendment guaranteeing suffrage to African American men

Academic Vocabulary

principle basic belief, rule, or law

Section Summary

OPPOSITION TO PRESIDENT JOHNSON

Almost as soon as the southern states created new legislatures, those legislatures went to work passing **Black Codes**. The Black Codes were laws that greatly limited the freedom of African Americans. In fact, the codes created working conditions that resembled slavery for African Americans. Many African Americans organized to protest codes.

The Black Codes angered many Republicans who believed the South was returning to its old ways. One group, known as the **Radical Republicans**, wanted the federal government to step in. They wanted more federal control over Reconstruction to make sure southern leaders did not remain loyal to the old Confederate **principles**. One Radical

> **What were Black Codes?**
> _____
> _____
> _____
> _____

Republican leader was Pennsylvania's Thaddeus Stevens. Stevens and others pushed for racial equality. They branded Johnson's plan a failure.

FOURTEENTH AMENDMENT

In 1866 Congress proposed a bill to give more power to the Freedmen's Bureau. President Johnson vetoed it. He believed Congress could not pass new laws until the South was represented in Congress.

Then Congress proposed the **Civil Rights Act of 1866**. It guaranteed African Americans the same legal rights as whites. Johnson vetoed this, too. Congress overrode the veto. It also proposed the **Fourteenth Amendment** to secure these protections.

CONGRESS TAKES CONTROL OF RECONSTRUCTION

After the 1866 elections, Republicans held a two-thirds majority in both the House and Senate. As a result, Congress passed several **Reconstruction Acts**. It also passed a law limiting the president's powers to remove cabinet members without Senate approval. When President Johnson broke that law by firing his secretary of war, Congress reacted by impeaching the president. The **impeachment** fell short by one vote. Johnson remained president, though he had little authority or influence.

FIFTEENTH AMENDMENT

Republicans believed that African Americans would support the Reconstruction plan. To gain their votes, Republicans in Congress proposed the **Fifteenth Amendment**, which guaranteed African American men the right to vote. This amendment went into effect in 1870.

CHALLENGE ACTIVITY

Critical Thinking: Research to Discover Find the Constitution in your textbook and read the Fourteenth and Fifteenth Amendments. Write a sentence paraphrasing each amendment.

> **Who believed President Johnson's Reconstruction plan was a failure?**
>
> _____
> _____
> _____
> _____

> **Why was President Johnson impeached?**
>
> _____
> _____
> _____
> _____

> **Which Americans gained the right to vote as a result of the Fifteenth Amendment?**
>
> _____
> _____

DIRECTIONS On the line provided before each statement, write **T** if a statement is true and **F** if a statement is false. If the statement is false, write the correct term on the line after each sentence that makes the sentence a true statement.

_____ 1. The <u>Civil Rights Act of 1866</u> provided African Americans with the same legal rights as white Americans.

_____

_____ 2. The <u>Fifteenth Amendment</u> gave all African American men throughout the United States the right to vote.

_____

_____ 3. The <u>Reconstruction Acts</u> were laws that restricted the overall freedom of African Americans.

_____

_____ 4. <u>Thaddeus Stevens</u> was a leader of the Radical Republicans who wanted economic justice for both African Americans and poor white southerners.

_____

_____ 5. The <u>Black Codes</u> were laws that divided the South into five districts with a military commander controlling each district.

_____

_____ 6. The <u>Radical Republicans</u> wanted the South to change much more than it already had before returning to the Union. They also felt that the Black Codes were cruel and unjust.

_____

_____ 7. The <u>Fourteenth Amendment</u> ensured citizenship for African Americans.

_____

Reconstruction

MAIN IDEAS
1. Reconstruction governments helped reform the South.
2. The Ku Klux Klan was organized as African Americans moved into positions of power.
3. As Reconstruction ended, the rights of African Americans were restricted.
4. Southern business leaders relied on industry to rebuild the South.

Key Terms and People

Hiram Revels first African American senator

Ku Klux Klan secret society that used violence to oppress African Americans

Compromise of 1877 agreement in which Democrats accepted Hayes's election to the presidency in exchange for removing federal troops form the South

poll tax special tax people had to pay before they could vote

segregation forced separation of whites and African Americans in public places

Jim Crow laws laws that enforced segregation

Plessy* v. *Ferguson Supreme Court ruling that upheld segregation

sharecropping system in which farm laborers kept some of the crop

Section Summary

RECONSTRUCTION GOVERNMENTS

After the Civil War, some northern Republicans moved to the South. They were not trusted by southerners who thought the Republicans had come to profit from Reconstruction. African Americans used their new right to vote to elect more than 600 African Americans, including the first black senator, **Hiram Revels**.

> **Who was the first African American senator?**
> _____
> _____
> _____
> _____

KU KLUX KLAN

Many southerners opposed Reconstruction. In 1866 a group created the secret and violent **Ku Klux Klan**. Its targets were African Americans, Republicans, and public officials. The Klan spread through the South until the federal government made Klan activities illegal. Violence, however, continued.

> **Circle the groups of Americans that were targeted by the Ku Klux Klan.**

RECONSTRUCTION ENDS

The General Amnesty Act of 1872 allowed most former Confederates to serve in public office. Soon many Democratic ex-Confederates were elected. Republicans also lost power as a result of Grant's problem-plagued presidency and the Panic of 1873. In 1876 the Hayes-Tilden presidential race was so close it took the **Compromise of 1877** to make sure Democats would accept Hayes's election.

Southern Democrats, called Redeemers, worked to limit African American rights. The methods they used included **poll taxes**, legal **segregation**, and **Jim Crow laws**. They even got help from the Supreme Court, which ruled in *Plessy* v. *Ferguson* that segregation was legal.

Rights were restricted in other ways, too. Most African Americans could not afford to buy land, so many began **sharecropping**. Often, the landowner profited, while sharecroppers lived in debt.

> Why did southern Republicans lose power during the 1870s?
> _____
> _____
> _____
> _____

REBUILDING INDUSTRY

The South's economy depended on cotton profits, which went up and down. In the "New South" movement, leaders turned to industry to strengthen the economy. Mills and factories were built. The new industries helped the southern economy grow.

> How was the economy of the "Old South" different from the economy of the "New South"?
> _____
> _____
> _____

RECONSTRUCTION IN THE NORTH

The effects of Reconstruction were not limited to groups in the South. Some Northern states passed laws that made segregation illegal. Racism didn't go away, however. Women's suffragists argued that women, like African Americans, should be granted equal rights. In 1869, Wyoming and Utah gave women the vote.

> Circle the states where women gained the right to vote.

CHALLENGE ACTIVITY

Critical Thinking: Write to Put in Sequence
Write a paragraph explaining how the General Amnesty Act led to the Compromise of 1877.

Guided Reading Workbook

DIRECTIONS Read each sentence and fill in the blank with the word in the word pair that best completes the sentence.

1. A special tax that people had to pay before they could vote was called a

_____. (poll tax/Jim Crow laws)

2. _____ was a system in which the landowners provided the land, tools, and supplies and workers provided the labor. (Segregation/Sharecropping)

3. In _____, the U.S. Supreme Court allowed segregation if "separate-but-equal" facilities were provided. (Compromise of 1877/*Plessy* v. *Ferguson*)

4. _____ was the first African American in the U.S. Senate. (Hiram Revels/James Alcorn)

5. The removal of remaining troops from the South, funding for internal

improvements, and the appointment of a southern Democrat to the president's

cabinet were part of the _____.

(Jim Crow laws/Compromise of 1877)

6. The forced separation of whites and African Americans in public places is called

_____. (segregation/Ku Klux Klan)

7. The _____ was a secret society that opposed civil rights for African Americans, and used violence and terror against African Americans. (Ku Klux Klan/Jim Crow laws)

8. _____ were common in southern states in the 1880s and enforced segregation. (Jim Crow laws/Segregationists)

Reconstruction

MAIN IDEAS

1. The U.S. government encouraged the settlement of the Great Plains.
2. Farms, ranches, and railroads were the basis of the economy that developed on the Plains.
3. Economic challenges led to the creation of farmers' political groups.
4. Native Americans and the U.S. government came into conflict over land in the West.

Key Terms and Places

Homestead Act federal law that gave government-owned land to small farmers

Morrill Act federal law that gave land to western states to encourage them to build colleges

Exodusters African Americans who settled in Kansas in the late 1800s

buffalo soldiers African American soldiers who served in the cavalry during the wars for the west

Dawes General Allotment Act federal law that split up Indian reservation land among individual Indians and promised them citizenship

Section Summary

NEW LIVES ON THE PLAINS

Many people moved west during the mid to late 1800s. The **Homestead Act** helped opened up land to settlers. The Act offered land plots to small farmers. Another law, the **Morrill Act,** gave land to states to sell. States had to build colleges with money they earned.

African Americans traveled west for the chance to own land and avoid discrimination. **Exodusters** were African Americans from the South who settled in Kansas. Other groups, including single women and immigrants from Europe, also moved west in search of opportunities.

What two government laws encouraged settlers to move west?

_____

_____

_____

_____

THE PLAINS ECONOMY

Most new settlers planned to farm. Farming on the Plains was very difficult. "Sodbusters" were farmers who worked hard to break through the tough sod, or land beneath the grass.

On the Plains, the cattle industry also grew. Farmers and ranchers competed for land that ranchers had once used for the open range.

The government encouraged the building of railroads stretching from east to west. By the 1890s, there were thousands of new train tracks. Railroads became one of the largest industries in the country.

The farming industry continued to expand. Soon farms produced more crops than could be sold. Farmers made less money. By the 1880s, many were working as tenant farmers. They had lost their farms and had to work on land owned by others.

> **Circle three industries that helped the Plains economy grow.**

CLASHES FOR THE WEST

Settlers and miners came into conflict over land with the Plains Indians. The U.S. government negotiated treaties to try to keep the peace. Over time, Native Americans lost more and more land. In 1861, treaties forced the Plains Indians to live on reservations. When some refused, the U.S. sent in troops, including African American cavalry the Native Americans called **buffalo soldiers.** Battles broke out throughout the Plains.

By the 1870s, many Native Americans were living on reservations. Children were often sent to schools to learn the customs of white people. Reformers called for changes. However, U.S. policy continued to reduce the influence of Indian traditions. The **Dawes General Allotment Act of 1887** made land ownership private. It divided up reservation land and gave some of it to individual Indians. The remaining land was kept or sold by the government. By the 1890s, the frontier was closed.

> **Why did fighting break out on the Great Plains?**
> _____
> _____
> _____
> _____

CHALLENGE ACTIVITY

Critical Thinking: Write to Persuade Create a brochure encouraging people to move west.

| Homestead Act | Exodusters | Dawes General Allotment Act |
| Morrill Act | buffalo soldiers | |

DIRECTIONS Answer each question by writing a sentence that contains at least one word from the word bank.

1. Which federal act divided Indian land into individual plots for Native

   Americans? _____

   _____

2. What name did Native Americans give to the African American cavalry who

   fought on the Great Plains? _____

   _____

3. Which federal act offered plots of land to small farmers?

   _____

   _____

4. What is the name for the African Americans who moved to Kansas from

   the South? _____

   _____

5. Which act required states to build colleges with profits from the sale of

   federal lands? _____

   _____